The Big Fearon
Dictionary & Library Skills Kit

Jeanne Hoffman & Elaine Prizzi

Fearon Teacher Aids
Carthage, Illinois

Illustrator: Duane Bibby

ISBN 0-8224-3055-X

Printed in the United States of America

1. 9 8 7 6

SEQUENCE OF UNITS

INTRODUCTION

Now combined for even greater convenience, Diction Harry and I.M.A. Booksnoop will supply you with all the necessary materials to teach dictionary and library skills.

This "kit between covers" contains 21 units each with objective statements, games, bulletin board ideas, reproducible worksheets, and mastery tests. The teacher's notes and answer keys complete this one-of-a-kind teaching resource.

Organized in an easy-to-use format, *The Big Fearon Dictionary & Library Skills Kit* covers the skills you teach!

PART I

Dictionary Skills

DICTION HARRY'S

Magical
Marvelous Motivating

DICTIONARY
SKILLS KIT

CONTENTS

INTRODUCTION

A kit in a book? You've got to be kidding! Where are all the cute little gizmos, workbooks, and teacher's guides that ordinarily make up a kit? Don't worry—it's all here, conveniently arranged in units, and complete with duplicatable worksheets featuring our own cute gizmo, the magical, marvelous motivator, Diction Harry. Here's what our "kit between covers" contains:

- A statement of objectives and classroom-management suggestions for each of nine dictionary skills units.
- Blackline masters for student worksheets in nine dictionary skills areas, adaptable for grades 4 through 8.
- Blackline masters for pretests, mastery tests, and reviews in each skills area and an overall mastery test.
- Interactive bulletin board ideas to provoke initial interest in each skills area.
- Learning games designed to reinforce skills.
- A Teacher's Notes section providing a statement of objectives, suggestions for use, and an answer key for the individual worksheets.

Unlike other kits, *Diction Harry's Magical, Marvelous, Motivating Dictionary Skills Kit* offers flexibility and economy. Multiple worksheets are offered in each unit, so you can select what you need for your particular teaching situation. The duplicatable masters prevent you from wasting money on fancy items that can be used only once. And *Diction Harry* is designed for convenience. Each page is perforated, allowing it to be detached easily and cleanly, and worksheets and teacher's notes are keyed to individual units for easy reference. And best of all, everything—absolutely *everything*—you need is conveniently packaged between these covers.

We strongly believe that the dictionary is the single most useful reference available to students and that students should learn to use the dictionary with ease and efficiency. We also believe that increased time spent on tasks increases students' learning and retention, and we have designed our worksheets accordingly. Moreover, we have made each worksheet a self-contained activity that students can work on without supervision to develop their independent work habits.

How to Use This Book

Pressed for time? Don't bother to read this section now. Go directly to the Unit 1 pretest for alphabetical ordering skills on page 11, remove the blackline master, send it through a thermofax, and run copies off a duplicating machine. Then come back to this section during your next coffee break.

Duplicating Masters

The duplicating (blackline) masters provide a complete, logical skill-development sequence for each unit: from pretest to introduction to extension to challenge to mastery test. After Unit 1, each worksheet requires the use of a dictionary.

- Use the worksheets in order.
- Skip the higher-level activities for less able or lower-level students.
- Consider the testing program optional. It is a convenient tool for gauging your students' levels of competence.
- Use a duplicating master as a transparency for a group activity if the material seems appropriate.

Unit Organization

The units themselves follow a logical skills-development sequence, beginning with the most basic skill, alphabetizing, and progressing to the most advanced skill, investigating etymologies. Each unit opens with a stated objective and a "before you begin" suggestion for overall unit management. These are followed by bulletin board ideas, games, and the duplicating masters.

- Introduce units that suit your particular group's needs and level. For example, if your fifth-graders have already mastered alphabetizing, you may want to begin with guide words; on the other hand, a group of slow readers may find phonetic keys too confusing to learn at present.
- Select activities within a unit that are appropriate for your students' abilities, or modify other activities. For example, if the vocabulary featured on a worksheet is too simple or too advanced, make changes accordingly.
- Introduce units by constructing their companion bulletin boards.
- Intersperse student work periods with correlated unit games.
- Use the suggestions for use in the teacher's notes to integrate various unit activities.

Meet the Magician.
Diction Harry

Our magician, Diction Harry, will make *you* a teaching magician! A poster featuring a caricature of Diction Harry is provided as a transparency master on page 5. Display him so that he becomes a familiar face that your students will recognize on their activity worksheets. Construct his hat and wand and use them as motivational props for games.

How to Make the Diction Harry Poster

Use a thermofax machine to make an overhead transparency of the blackline master provided on page 5. Project the transparency onto a large sheet of paper, tagboard, or poster board. Trace the projected outline with a pencil or felt-tip pen; then color in the caricature or have your students color it in. Display the poster prominently, and refer to it as you introduce each new unit.

How to Make Diction Harry's Magic Wand

MATERIALS
- black tagboard or wooden dowel
- stapler or tape (for tagboard)
- black paint (for dowel)

PROCEDURE
1. Cut a 2-by-18-inch rectangle out of black tagboard.
2. Roll the rectangle into a long cylinder about 1 inch in diameter.
3. Staple or tape the overlapping edges.
OR
4. Procure a dowel and paint it black.

How to Make Diction Harry's Hat

MATERIALS

- black tagboard
- stapler or tape (optional)
- white glue

PROCEDURE

1. Cut out the three hat pieces from black tagboard as shown in Figure 1.

2. Score the rim and crown and make slits as shown in Figure 2.

3. Gently roll the body into a cylinder and glue, staple, or tape the edges in place as shown in Figure 3.

4. Put the hat pieces together as shown in Figure 4. First, fold up the tabs on the rim. Apply glue to the outside surfaces of the tabs, place the cylinder over the rim, and press the tabs firmly against the inside of the cylinder.

5. Bend the tabs on the crown so that they are at right angles to the edge. Apply glue to the outside surfaces of the tabs and press them firmly against the inside of the cylinder. No tabs should show on the outside of the hat. (See Figure 5.)

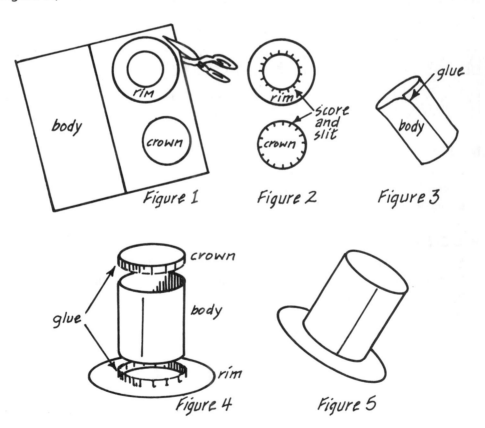

Figure 1   Figure 2   Figure 3

Figure 4   Figure 5

Unit 1

Alphabetizing

Objective

The students will alphabetize words using the first, second, third, and subsequent letters as needed.

Before You Begin

Check your students' mastery of the alphabet and of alphabetizing by administering the unit pretest on page 11. Your students must know the alphabet to be successful in this unit and the units that follow; the duplicating masters will develop their skills in alphabetizing by the first, second, third, and subsequent letters.

Bulletin Board
ABC Tree Houses

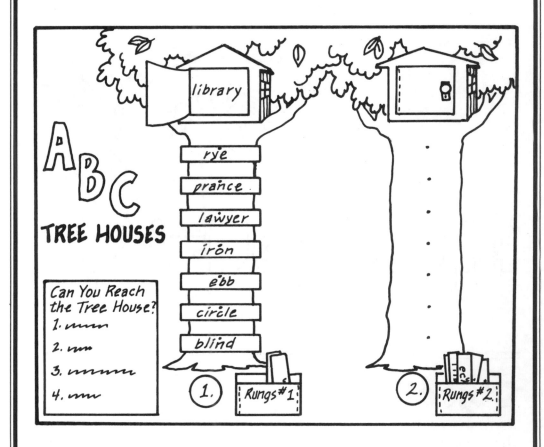

OBJECTIVE The students will use their alphabetizing skills to complete the bulletin board.

DESCRIPTION The rungs of the tree house ladders are cards with words printed on them. The student places the cards in alphabetical order on the ladder. If the student is correct, the second letters of the words spell two secret words.

SUGGESTIONS FOR USE Use this bulletin board after administering the Alphabetizing Pretest.

MATERIALS
- construction paper
- hole punch
- tagboard
- felt-tip pen
- pushpins
- stapler

PROCEDURE

1. Make the trees and tree houses from construction paper and staple them in position on the bulletin board.

2. Print the secret words *library* and *dictionary* behind the tree house doors.

3. Cut seventeen tagboard strips as rungs for the tree house ladders and print one of the following words on each rung: blind, circle, ebb, iron, lawyer, prance, rye (these words spell *library*); addle, diet, echo, item, lilac, modern, onion, paste, trade, Wyoming (these words spell *dictionary*).

4. Punch a hole in the top center of each rung.

5. Prepare the caption and staple it in position on the bulletin board.

6. Make two pockets from two pieces of 8½-by-11-inch construction paper. Fold up the bottom of each piece to one inch from the top and staple the sides to form a pocket. Label the pockets Rungs #1 and Rungs #2. Staple the pockets in position on the bulletin board. Put the appropriate pack of cards in each pocket.

7. Print the following directions on a piece of construction paper and staple it in position on the board:

Can You Reach the Tree House?

1. Take the word cards from the pocket.
2. Place them in alphabetical order from the bottom up.
3. If you are correct, the second letters of the words will spell a secret word. Check the secret word behind the tree house door.
4. Return the word cards to the correct pocket.

Game
Alphabet Questions

OBJECTIVE The students will use their knowledge of the alphabet to discover secret letters.

DESCRIPTION This game is similar to Twenty Questions. A secret letter is drawn and the players try to guess its identity.

SUGGESTIONS FOR USE Use this game to get your dictionary unit off to a good start. The types of questions your students ask will give you valuable clues to the students' levels of mastery. The deductive logic needed will sharpen their thinking skills, too.

MATERIALS

- Diction Harry's Magic Hat and Wand
- 26 index cards, each with a letter of the alphabet on it

PROCEDURE

1. Place the alphabet cards in the hat.

2. Introduce Diction Harry and his magic hat and wand to the group.

3. Explain the rules of the game:

   a. The object of the game is to guess the secret letter.

   b. A student waves the wand and draws a card out of the hat without letting anyone see it, reads the letter on it, and puts it aside, face down.

   c. The other players can ask a total of seven questions that can be answered either Yes or No. The teacher will keep track of the number of questions asked. (Point out to the students that it is better to use strategic questions, such as "Is the letter before *M*?", if they do not do so on their own.)

   d. The player who guesses correctly draws the next card.

Alphabetizing Pretest

A. Write the alphabet in the spaces below.

A __ __ __ __ __ __ __ __ __ __ __ __

__ __ __ __ __ __ __ __ __ __ __ __ Z

B. Write the next three letters of the alphabet that follow each letter below.

1. d e f g   3. h ___ ___ ___

2. m ___ ___ ___   4. s ___ ___ ___

C. Number the words in each list below in alphabetical order.

1. ___ menu   2. ___ coffee
   1 able   ___ city
   ___ sample   ___ camera
   ___ decide   ___ cymbal
   ___ vase   ___ certain

3. ___ frame   4. ___ plank
   ___ fry   ___ planet
   ___ free   ___ plant
   ___ froth   ___ plankton
   ___ fright   ___ plane

NAME _____

Sing a Song of 26-Pence!

A. Fill in the letters of the alphabet that come just before and just after each letter below.

1. B c D
2. __ R __
3. __ L __
4. __ F __
5. __ X __
6. __ P __

7. __ U __
8. __ D __
9. __ K __
10. __ T __
11. __ B __
12. __ N __

13. __ Y __
14. __ S __
15. __ G __
16. __ Q __
17. __ I __
18. __ M __

19. __ H __
20. __ E __
21. __ O __
22. __ V __
23. __ J __
24. __ W __

B. Write the next three letters of the alphabet that follow each letter below.

1. d e f g
2. r __ __ __
3. b __ __ __
4. j __ __ __

5. w __ __ __
6. m __ __ __
7. h __ __ __
8. c __ __ __

9. f __ __ __
10. s __ __ __
11. g __ __ __
12. o __ __ __

C. Number the words in each list below in alphabetical order.

1. __ come
   __ earn
   __ jolly
   __ deer
   __ flag

2. __ plan
   __ idle
   __ lake
   __ queen
   __ order

3. __ zebra
   __ unit
   __ wax
   __ sailor
   __ rust

12 Diction Harry

Diction Harry reproducible page, copyright © 1983

Marching in Alphabet Time

A. Write the words below in alphabetical order. Place a check next to each word in the list after you write it.

even	carry	since	knew	quick
because	hitch	grin	teach	young
much	pencil	feel	least	which
after	interest	jungle	race	very
xylophone	never	often	zoo	until
dense				

1. _____   10. _____   19. _____

2. _____   11. _____   20. _____

3. _____   12. _____   21. _____

4. _____   13. _____   22. _____

5. _____   14. _____   23. _____

6. _____   15. _____   24. _____

7. _____   16. _____   25. _____

8. _____   17. _____   26. _____

9. _____   18. _____

B. In each pair of words below, underline the letters that you use to help you decide which word comes first in alphabetical order. Then circle the word that comes first.

1. ship *or* stop   3. some *or* same   5. divide *or* does

2. piece *or* paper   4. climb *or* come   6. trail *or* time

C. Number the words in each list in alphabetical order. Use the second letter in each word.

1. ___ best   2. ___ pie   3. ___ under

   ___ bacon   ___ purple   ___ useful

   ___ bin   ___ pan   ___ upper

Alphabetizing 13

The Alphabet Two-Step and Others

A. Number the words in each list below in alphabetical order. Use the second letter in each word.

1. ___ city   2. ___ single   3. ___ medium

   ___ camera   ___ scale   ___ mighty

   ___ cedar   ___ speak   ___ main

   ___ cycle   ___ slope   ___ music

   ___ cheese   ___ saddle   ___ .mystery

B. Write the words in each list below in alphabetical order. Use the third letter in each word.

1. try   2. chain   3. plum
   train   chin   plenty
   trim   cheer   play
   tree   chum   plot

_____   _____   _____

_____   _____   _____

_____   _____   _____

_____   _____   _____

C. Sometimes you need to look at the fourth or even the fifth letters of words to decide on the correct alphabetical order of the words. Number the words in each list below in alphabetical order.

1. ___ speaker   2. ___ tremble   3. ___ birdseed   4. ___ horseshoe

   ___ special   ___ tread   ___ birth   ___ horn

   ___ speedy   ___ trend   ___ birdbath   ___ horseman

   ___ speckle   ___ treat   ___ birdhouse   ___ horrible

Diction Harry reproducible page, copyright © 1983

NAME _____

The Jumbo Jumble

A. Can you unscramble this giant list of *j* words? Write the words in alphabetical order. Place a check next to each word in the list after you write it.

jewel	jack	jungle	junior
jester	jumper	jingle	jet engine
jute	jet plane	justice	jackpot
jade	jostle	jut	jelly
January	junk	jaw	jellyfish

1. _____   11. _____

2. _____   12. _____

3. _____   13. _____

4. _____   14. _____

5. _____   15. _____

6. _____   16. _____

7. _____   17. _____

8. _____   18. _____

9. _____   19. _____

10. _____ 20. _____

B. What do the words below have in <u>common</u>? Number the words in alphabetical order. Use the fourth, fifth, sixth, and seventh letters.

____ commission   ____ commodity

____ commutative   ____ commoner

____ community   ____ commerce

____ commence   ____ commentary

____ committee   ____ commitment

Diction Harry reproducible page, copyright © 1983

Alphabetizing 15

Mystery Messages

A. Decode the message below by substituting the letter in the alphabet that comes *before* each letter in the message.

U I F   T F D P O E

___ ___ ___   ___ ___ ___ ___ ___ ___

N Z T U F S Z   D B O   C F

___ ___ ___ ___ ___ ___ ___   ___ ___ ___   ___ ___

T P M W F E   C Z

___ ___ ___ ___ ___ ___   ___ ___

M P P L J O H   V O E F S

___ ___ ___ ___ ___ ___ ___   ___ ___ ___ ___ ___

U I F   E J D U J P O B S Z

___ ___ ___   ___ ___ ___ ___ ___ ___ ___ ___ ___ ___

P O   Z P V S

___ ___   ___ ___ ___ ___

U F B D I F S ' T   E F T L.

___ ___ ___ ___ ___ ___ ___ ' ___   ___ ___ ___ ___.

Diction Harry reproducible page, copyright © 1983

Mystery Messages *continued*

B.

B N M F Q Z S T K Z S H N M R!

_ _ _ _ _ _ _ _ _ _ _ _ _ _ _!

X N T   G Z U D   M N V

_ _ _   _ _ _ _   _ _ _

V N M   S G D   S H S K D

_ _ _   _ _ _   _ _ _ _ _

N E   L Z R S D Q

_ _   _ _ _ _ _ _

C D B N C D Q   N E   S G D

_ _ _ _ _ _ _   _ _   _ _ _

T M H S D C   R S Z S D R

_ _ _ _ _ _   _ _ _ _ _ _

R D B Q D S   R D Q U H B D!

_ _ _ _ _ _   _ _ _ _ _ _ _!

X N T Q   S D Z B G D Q

_ _ _ _   _ _ _ _ _ _ _

G Z R   X N T Q   A Z C F D.

_ _ _   _ _ _ _   _ _ _ _ _.

Mystery Messages *continued*

C. The code below has a different pattern. To help you figure it out, the first two words of the message have been decoded. List the letters of the alphabet on the first line below and fill in the code on the second line as you discover it.

_____

_____

A W S   R P Y S P A L I   L G

T h e   i n v e n t o r __ __

A W S   A S O S F I T N W,

___ ___ ___   ___ ___ ___ ___ ___ ___ ___ ___,

E T C X S O   C L I E S,

___ ___ ___ ___ ___ ___   ___ ___ ___ ___,

T O E L   B S Y S O L N S B

___ ___ ___ ___   ___ ___ ___ ___ ___ ___ ___ ___

A W S   C L I E S   M L B S,

___ ___ ___   ___ ___ ___ ___ ___   ___ ___ ___ ___,

H W R M W   X E S E

___ ___ ___ ___ ___   ___ ___ ___ ___

B L A E,   B T E W S E,   T P B

___ ___ ___ ___,   ___ ___ ___ ___ ___ ___,   ___ ___ ___

E N T M S E

___ ___ ___ ___ ___ ___.

Alphabetizing Mastery Test

A. Write the words below in alphabetical order.

animal	parrot	canary	camel	gnu
koala bear	zebra	hyena	tiger	monkey

1. _____   6. _____

2. _____   7. _____

3. _____   8. _____

4. _____   9. _____

5. _____   10. _____

B. Circle the word that comes first alphabetically in each pair below.

1. coat *or* canoe

2. plank *or* place

3. birth *or* birch

4. marry *or* merry

5. cable *or* cackle

6. injury *or* injustice

7. hawk *or* hammer

8. Indian *or* index

9. table *or* tackle

10. metal *or* medal

11. message *or* messenger

12. perspire *or* perspiration

C. Number the words in each list below in alphabetical order.

1. ___ cull

___ crime

___ chair

___ cane

___ cease

___ comma

2. ___ pry

___ prune

___ prose

___ pray

___ press

___ prey

3. ___ stray

___ strange

___ stream

___ strainer

___ strand

___ strain

Unit 2

Guide Words

Objective

The students will review, use, and extend their skills in using guide words to locate dictionary entries.

Before You Begin

Be sure your students have mastered alphabetizing. Administer the pretest on page 24. Use the results of the pretest to determine the students' instructional needs.

Bulletin Board
Sky Ride to Guide Words

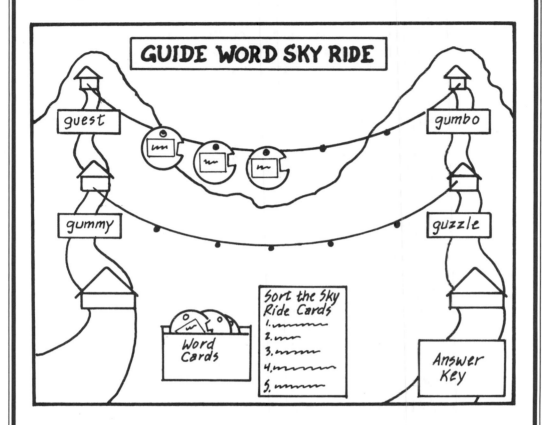

OBJECTIVE The students will use their knowledge of the use of guide words to complete the bulletin board.

DESCRIPTION The students sort sky-ride word cards according to guide words provided.

SUGGESTIONS FOR USE Use this bulletin board to demonstrate how guide words function in a dictionary and to reinforce alphabetizing skills from the previous unit.

MATERIALS

- construction paper, assorted colors
- stapler
- scissors
- tagboard
- hole punch
- pen
- yarn
- pushpins

PROCEDURE

1. Staple sky-blue construction paper onto the top half of the bulletin board.

2. Cut out two mountains from white, light brown, or light green construction paper. Staple them in position, overlapping near the bottom, on the bulletin board.

3. Make the sky-ride terminals out of contrasting construction paper and staple them in position on the board.

4. Make a pattern for the sky-ride word cards and cut 10 cards from tagboard. Punch a hole in the top center of each card so that it can be hung from a pushpin.

5. Print the words to be sorted on the sky-ride word cards. (See the word lists below.)

6. Cut out four guide word signs from tagboard.

7. Print the guide words on the signs.

8. Staple the signs and yarn in position on the bulletin board.

9. Place five pushpins at equal intervals along each strand of yarn.

10. Prepare the caption and staple it in position on the board.

11. Prepare a pocket for the sky-ride word cards. Fold an 8½-by-11-inch piece of construction paper to within one inch from the top and staple along the sides. Staple the pocket in position on the bulletin board and put the sky-ride word cards in the pocket.

12. Make an answer key. Fold an 8½-by-11-inch piece of construction paper in half. Print Answer Key on the front. Lift the flap and print the answers inside. Staple the answer key in position on the board.

13. Print the following directions on an 8½-by-11-inch piece of construction paper:

Sort the Sky Ride Cards

1. Take the cards from the pocket.
2. Read the word on each card and decide which pair of guide words it goes with.
3. Hang the cards on the correct sky-ride lines.
4. Check your answers by lifting the answer key flap.
5. Replace the sky-ride word cards when you are finished.

WORD LISTS

1. *Guide words:* kangaroo *and* kettle; key *and* kilogram. *Words:* kayak, keel, keen, keep, kennel, keyboard, kick, kid, kidney, kiln

2. *Guide words:* rabbit *and* radar; radiate *and* rain. *Words:* rabble, raccoon, race, racket, radar, radio, radish, rage, raid, rail

Game
Guide Word Relay

OBJECTIVE The students will use their knowledge of the use of guide words to complete lists of words.

DESCRIPTION Teams compete, relay fashion, to be the first to complete a list of words that would be found on a dictionary page with a specified set of guide words.

SUGGESTIONS FOR USE The students will be ready for this game after they complete the activity featured on the Sky Ride to Guide Words bulletin board. Use this game later to review guide words.

MATERIALS
- chalkboard, chart paper, or an overhead projector to display a set of guide words and a master list of word choices
- paper and pencil for each team

PROCEDURE
1. Prepare the game lists. (See below.)
2. Divide the group into teams, with a maximum of six players per team.
3. Arrange the teams in rows.
4. Provide the first player of each team with a piece of paper and a pencil.
5. Explain the rules:
   a. The object of the game is to find the words that belong on the dictionary page indicated by the given guide words.
   b. The first player writes a word from the master list that belongs on the page designated by the guide words given and passes the paper and pencil to the next player.
   c. The second player must write a different word that belongs on the page, and so on.
   d. The last player stands when he or she is finished.
   e. If a player finds an error made by a previous team member, the player may correct it.
   f. The first team to complete a list correctly is the winner.

GAME LISTS (correct answers in bold)
   1. *Guide words:*   dash   dazzle
Master list: **daze, daytime,** dandy, dance, **dawn,** dare, **dashing,** dark, **daydream,** deadlock, daring, **daughter**
   2. *Guide words:*   neck   neglect
Master list: **nectar, needy,** neat, **negative,** nerve, **need,** necessity, **neckline,** near, neighbor, **needle,** never
   3. *Guide words:*   stretcher   strive
Master list: **stride,** stretch, **strikeout, stricken,** strap, **stripe,** stroll, strength, **strike, string,** stroke, stress
   4. *Guide words:*   precious   prepare
Master list: precaution, **prejudice,** prepay, **prefix, precise,** precede, prescribe, **prefer,** preposition, **predict, precipitate,** preserve
   5. *Guide words:*   commend   commotion
Master list: comfort, commence, **commission, commend,** community, company, communicate, **common, commotion,** command, **commercial, commode**

Guide Words Pretest

A. Put a check beside each sentence below that is true.

___ 1. Guide words are found at the top of a dictionary page.

___ 2. Guide words will help you find words in the dictionary more quickly.

___ 3. The word you are looking for will be found after the second guide word.

___ 4. The guide words for <u>basket</u> could be <u>basin</u> and <u>bass</u>.

B. The guide words for a dictionary page are <u>jack</u> and <u>jewel</u>. Circle the words below that you would find on the page.

1. jam
2. jazz
3. jetty
4. jerky
5. June

6. jabber
7. jacket
8. just
9. jab
10. jade

C. Find each word below in your dictionary. Write the guide words that are on the page for each word.

1. baseball _____ and _____

2. carpenter _____ and _____

3. towel _____ and _____

Front, Middle, or Back?

A. What are the three sections of your dictionary? Use the pictures to fill in the blanks.

1. Front	2. Middle	3. Back
Letters ___ to ___	Letters ___ to ___	Letters ___ to ___

Knowing the letters in the three parts of the dictionary will help you find things fast!

B. Practice thinking of the dictionary in three parts. Write *front*, *middle*, or *back* to tell which part of your dictionary you would use to find each word below.

1. tadpole _____
2. barracuda _____
3. loophole _____
4. spring _____
5. coverall _____

6. goggle _____
7. radio _____
8. pasture _____
9. intern _____
10. voyage _____

C. Practice using your dictionary. To find tadpole, you would use the back of your dictionary. Try to open your dictionary to the section that has words beginning with *t*. If you find *s* words or *u* words, you are very close!

D. Try to open your dictionary to the *b* words to find barracuda. Put a check beside barracuda in the list above if you found the *b*-words section on the first try. Do this with each of the words in the list above.

NAME _____

Take Me to Your Leader!

A. Use your dictionary to answer these questions.

Turn to page 175. What is the first word listed? (1) _____

The last word? (2) _____ The guide words for this page are

(3) _____ and (4) _____. The left-hand guide word

is always the (5) _____ word on the page, and the right-

hand guide word is always the (6) _____ word on the page.

B. Find the page number and guide words in your dictionary for each word listed below. Complete the chart by writing the numbers and words.

Page	First Guide Word	Word	Second Guide Word
457	square knot	squaw	stabilizing
1.		shimmer	
2.		robot	
3.		corner	
4.		opinion	
5.		suit	
6.		squirm	
7.		gasoline	
8.		panic	
9.		mayor	
10.		alter	

C. Extra for Experts: Use your dictionary to find 10 interesting words that begin with the letter *b.* List them on a piece of paper in any order. Challenge a friend to number them in alphabetical order.

26 Diction Harry

Finding Words Fast

Always look at the guide words before you scan the dictionary page for your word.

A. Use your dictionary to find the guide words for the words listed below.

1. neon _____ and _____

2. energy _____ and _____

3. solar _____ and _____

4. fireplace _____ and _____

5. storeroom _____ and _____

6. machine _____ and _____

7. bridle _____ and _____

8. garnet _____ and _____

9. geometry _____ and _____

10. pilgrim _____ and _____

B. The guide words for a dictionary page are <u>skim</u> and <u>slam</u>. Circle the words below that you would find on the page.

1. skin	6. slack	11. sew
2. swim	7. slope	12. skit
3. sack	8. slab	13. stir
4. skip	9. slash	14. skyline
5. skipper	10. skull	15. sketch

From Sheathe to Shield

A. The guide words for a dictionary page are <u>sheathe</u> and <u>shield</u>. In the list below, tell which words would be found before the page, on the page, or after the page. Write *before, on,* or *after* next to each word.

1. shepherd _____
2. shelf _____
3. sheen _____
4. shore _____
5. she _____
6. shed _____
7. shellac _____
8. sheep _____
9. shame _____
10. scarf _____
11. sheik _____
12. shift _____
13. shave _____
14. sunny _____
15. sharpen _____

16. short _____
17. shingle _____
18. shield _____
19. sew _____
20. shears _____
21. sheriff _____
22. sheer _____
23. shark _____
24. slumber _____
25. shimmer _____
26. sheet _____
27. shatter _____
28. shock _____
29. shade _____
30. sheepskin _____

B. Challenge: Number the words in the list above in alphabetical order.

C. Extra for Experts: The words *shield* and *sheathe* make you think of a knight in shining armor. Use your dictionary to find out about these other pieces of armor worn by a medieval knight: gauntlet, chain mail, beaver, gorget, and solleret.

Guide Words Mastery Test

A. The guide words for a dictionary page are <u>cell</u> and <u>crab</u>. Circle the words below that you would find on the page.

1. celery	6. crop	11. change	16. crack
2. circle	7. crunch	12. century	17. count
3. click	8. center	13. charm	18. common
4. cycle	9. cream	14. cedar	19. cell
5. craft	10. channel	15. cellar	20. crabpot

B. Read each sentence carefully. Fill in each blank with the best word or words. Spell carefully!

1. Words in the dictionary are listed in _____ order.

2. The left-hand guide word is the _____ word on that page, and the right-hand guide word is the

   _____ word on that page.

3. To find a certain word quickly, always look at the

   _____ first.

Diction Harry reproducible page, copyright © 1983

Unit 3

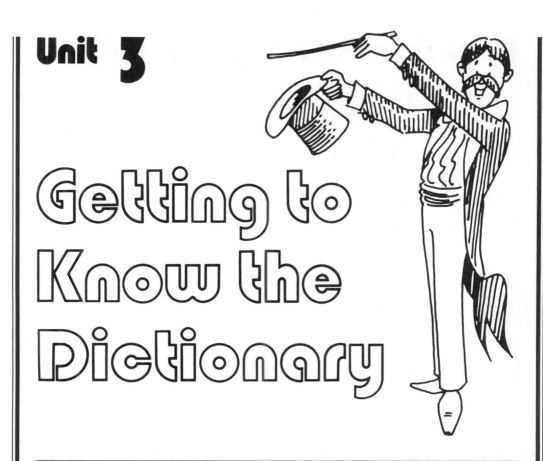

Getting to Know the Dictionary

Objective

The students will become familiar with the scope and limitations of a dictionary.

Before You Begin

Check your students' knowledge of what is in a dictionary by administering the unit pretest on page 35. The duplicating masters in this unit may be used at any time that you feel your students are using guide words correctly.

Bulletin Board
Ask the Crystal Ball

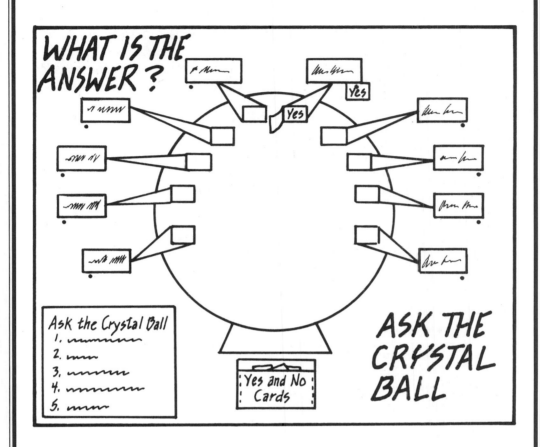

OBJECTIVE The students will use their knowledge of the scope and limitations of a dictionary.

DESCRIPTION The crystal ball gives the correct answers to questions about the scope and limitations of a dictionary.

SUGGESTIONS FOR USE Use this bulletin board at any stage in your students' skill development. Use it to motivate, extend, or review skills.

MATERIALS
- tagboard
- construction paper
- scissors
- felt-tip pen
- hole punch
- stapler
- pushpins

PROCEDURE

1. Cut ten 6-by-10-inch tagboard cards and print a question on each card. (See the list of suggested questions below.)

2. Prepare the crystal ball. Cut a large circle, sized to fit your bulletin board, from white tagboard or construction paper. Cut 10 doors in the crystal ball.

3. Cut a matching circle from paper whose color harmonizes with your bulletin board's color scheme.

4. Place the crystal ball on top of the matching circle. Arrange the question cards around the crystal ball and print the appropriate Yes or No answer behind each door.

5. Cut 10 rays from yellow construction paper.

6. Cut ten 3-by-5 inch cards. Print Yes on five cards and No on the other five cards. Punch a hole in the top center of each card so it can be hung from a pushpin.

7. Position the crystal ball, the rays, and the question cards on the board. Place a pushpin beside each question card.

8. Make a pocket to hold the Yes and No cards. Fold a piece of 8½-by-11-inch construction paper to within one inch from the top and staple the sides to form a pocket. Print Yes and No Cards on the pocket. Position the pocket on the bulletin board.

9. Print the following directions on a piece of construction paper and position it on the board:

Ask the Crystal Ball

1. Read a question.
2. Decide Yes or No.
3. Show your answer by hanging a Yes or a No card on the pushpin.
4. Follow the ray to the answer door on the crystal ball and check your answer.
5. Close the doors and return the Yes and No cards when finished.

QUESTION LIST* (answers in bold)

1. Are the most important words listed first in a dictionary? **No**
2. Might a dictionary tell the language that gave us a certain word? **Yes**
3. Is there a list of abbreviations in your dictionary? **Yes**
4. Is stopping listed by itself? **No**
5. Does the dictionary have pictures to explain meanings? **Yes**
6. Can the dictionary tell you where George Washington lived? **No**
7. Will the dictionary help you spell squirrel correctly? **Yes**
8. Is there a short pronunciation key at the top of each dictionary page? **No**
9. Are easy words, such as go and run, left out of a dictionary? **No**
10. Will the dictionary tell you how to spell unusual plurals? **Yes**
11. Are all the words in the English language listed in a dictionary? **No**
12. Do the phonetic spellings tell you how to pronounce words? **Yes**
13. Does your dictionary give the meanings of proper nouns? **Yes**
14. Are synonyms and antonyms listed for all words? **No**
15. Does an accent mark tell you which syllable to stress? **Yes**

*Verify the answers with the dictionaries you will use.

Game
The Magic Book

OBJECTIVE The students will discover some of the ways a dictionary is helpful.

DESCRIPTION The students compete to be the first to find answers to questions regarding specific ways of using a dictionary.

SUGGESTIONS FOR USE Use this game to introduce Unit 3. The game questions cover the main aspects of when and why to use a dictionary. Review the use of the front, middle, and back sections of a dictionary.

MATERIALS

- Diction Harry's magic hat and wand
- dictionary for each player
- 12 or more 5-by-7-inch index cards
- felt-tip pen

PROCEDURE

1. Prepare the question cards. Print a question that requires students to make specific use of the dictionary on one side of a card and the word keyed to the question on the other side. (See the list of game questions below.)
2. Place the question cards in Diction Harry's hat.
3. Have each player take a dictionary.
4. Explain the rules:
    a. A card will be picked from the hat, and the word on the card will be read or written on the chalkboard.
    b. When the leader says "Go!" you may open your dictionaries and begin looking for the word.
    c. When all players have located the word, the question will be read aloud.
    d. The player who answers the question correctly gets to wave the magic wand and pick the next card.
5. Summarize the facets of a dictionary by showing each card again and listing each use on the chalkboard.

QUESTION LIST

Usage	Side One	Side Two
1. Pronunciation	How do you say this word?	phoebe
2. Spelling	Is this the correct spelling?	petroleum
3. Meanings of words	What does this word mean?	bide
4. Unusual plurals (shown)	What is the plural of this word?	phenomenon

5. Regular plurals (not shown)	What is the plural of this word?	jet ✓
6. How to write compound words	How do you write this word?	ice cream, ice-cream, ✓ or icecream
7. Finding synonyms	Find a synonym for this word.	say
8. Meanings of prefixes and suffixes	Find the meaning of this suffix.	-ful ✓
9. Part of speech and correct usage	What part of speech is given first for this word? Second?	tack ✓
10. Principal parts of verbs	Find the verb entry. What are the principal parts?	swim
11. Pictures and derivations	What else does the dictionary show to help you understand this word?	~~iris~~ Kinkajou
12. Other helpful information	What type of word is this? Find the place where this is listed.	bldg. ✓

Getting to Know the Dictionary Pretest

A. What kinds of information are in a dictionary? Write *yes* beside each item below that you would find in a standard dictionary.

_____ 1. Meanings of words

_____ 2. Pronunciations of words

_____ 3. Synonyms for words

_____ 4. Meanings of prefixes

_____ 5. Parts of speech for words

_____ 6. How to use words in sentences correctly

_____ 7. The history of basketball

_____ 8. How to write compound words

_____ 9. How to divide words into syllables

_____ 10. How George Washington was elected the first president of the United States

B. Write *yes* next to each question that you would be able to find an answer to in your dictionary.

_____ 1. What is the meaning of <u>diligent</u>?

_____ 2. When will Halley's Comet <u>reappear</u>?

_____ 3. Is this the correct spelling of <u>excellent</u>?

_____ 4. Where is <u>Timbuctoo</u>?

Diction Harry reproducible page, copyright © 1983

Meet Your Dictionary

A. Turn to the table of contents in your dictionary. Answer the questions below. Write your answers.

_____ 1. On which page in the dictionary do the spelling rules begin?

_____ 2. Does your dictionary have a separate list of abbreviations?

_____ 3. Does your dictionary have a list of signs and symbols?

_____ 4. Turn to the list of signs and symbols and copy the zodiac sign for <u>Taurus</u>.

B. Explore your dictionary to answer the questions below. Write your answers.

_____ 1. On which page do words beginning with <u>c</u> start?

_____ 2. On which page is the word <u>skate</u>?

_____ 3. How many pages in the dictionary have words beginning with <u>x</u>?

_____ 4. Which letter has more pages, <u>e</u> or <u>t</u>?

_____ 5. Find a word listed in the <u>ds</u> that has an illustration. Write the word.

C. Extra for Experts: Dig deeper to find these answers.

_____ 1. Which letter has the fewest pages?

_____ 2. Name a nation in Africa that begins with the letter <u>T</u>.

_____ 3. Who was the first vice-president of the United States?

_____ 4. Make up a dictionary question of your own to ask your classmates.

_____

_____

Investigate Your Dictionary

A. Use your dictionary to find each underlined item below. Then answer each question.

1. What is the correct spelling of <u>possable</u>? _____

2. How is <u>dynamic</u> divided into syllables? _____

3. What is the plural of <u>sheaf</u>? _____

4. What is one meaning of <u>jib</u>? _____

5. What is a synonym for <u>thrive</u>? _____

6. What does the prefix <u>re-</u> mean? _____

7. What is the pronunciation for <u>gauge</u>? _____

8. What part of speech is <u>tine</u>? _____

9. What is the abbreviation for <u>brothers</u>? _____

10. What are the other two forms of the verb <u>zip</u>? _____

    and _____

11. What is one symbol for <u>and</u>? _____

12. What language gave us the word <u>cycle</u>? _____

B. Extra for Experts: Mary Poppins introduced us to *supercalifragilisticexpialidocious*. It's not the longest word in our language. *Pneumonoultramicroscopicsilicovolcanoconiosis* has 45 letters. List some long words you can find in your dictionary. Write the meaning of each word.

Word	Meaning
_____	_____
_____	_____
_____	_____
_____	_____

SOS

A. Help! What do these abbreviations stand for? Write the letter of each abbreviation below in the blank next to its meaning. Some abbreviations have more than one meaning. You may use your dictionary.

Meaning

_____ 1. mountain

_____ 2. East

_____ 3. Save our souls! (international distress signal)

_____ 4. Her/His Majesty's ship

_____ 5. street

_____ 6. British thermal unit

_____ 7. lieutenant

_____ 8. treasurer

_____ 9. temperature

_____ 10. English

_____ 11. Saint

_____ 12. cash on delivery

_____ 13. corporal

_____ 14. temporary

Abbreviation

a. SOS
b. St.
c. treas.
d. mt.

e. E
f. Cpl.
g. Lt.
h. COD

i. HMS
j. Btu.
k. temp.

B. How many abbreviations for states' names do you know? Can you list all 50? Try it!

_____ _____ _____ _____ _____ _____

_____ _____ _____ _____ _____ _____

_____ _____ _____ _____ _____ _____

_____ _____ _____ _____ _____ _____

_____ _____ _____ _____ _____ _____

_____ _____ _____ _____ _____ _____

_____

Would You Eat a Jitney?

A. Use your dictionary to find the meaning of each underlined word below. Then answer each question.

1. Does a <u>florin</u> have flowers? _____

2. Would a pet shop have a lot of <u>petioles</u>? _____

3. With what would you like to <u>bedizen</u> yourself? _____

   _____

4. Is a <u>thole</u> a large mole? _____

5. Would it surprise you to find a person in a <u>crow's nest</u>? _____

6. Would the president of the United States <u>declaim</u>? _____

7. Does your birthday come on the <u>ides</u> of any month? _____

8. Did you ever use an <u>egress</u>? _____

9. What is your <u>sobriquet</u>? _____

10. Would you be pleased if someone gave you some <u>asafetida</u>?

    _____

B. Extra for Experts: Find five interesting words that are new to you. Fill in the chart below.

Page	Word	Meaning
_____	_____	_____
_____	_____	_____
_____	_____	_____
_____	_____	_____
_____	_____	_____

Getting to Know the Dictionary Mastery Test

A. Read each statement below. Then write *true* or *false* in the blanks.

_____ 1. A dictionary can help you check the spelling of a word.

_____ 2. Many dictionaries have special lists, such as spelling rules, abbreviations, and cities of the world.

_____ 3. The plural of the word <u>dog</u> will be listed in your dictionary.

_____ 4. Your dictionary will help you learn to pronounce a word.

_____ 5. Easy words, such as <u>doll</u> and <u>come</u>, are not in a dictionary.

_____ 6. The dictionary will tell you the history of football.

_____ 7. <u>Play</u> and <u>played</u> will be listed in your dictionary.

_____ 8. Entries are listed alphabetically.

_____ 9. Many words have more than one meaning.

_____ 10. Your dictionary will tell you if a word is a noun, a verb, or another part of speech.

B. Name two special sections of your dictionary.

_____

_____

Diction Harry reproducible page, copyright © 1983

Unit 4

Understanding Dictionary Entries

Objective

The students will become familiar with the parts of a dictionary entry and the function of each part.

Before You Begin

Give the pretest on page 47. Unit 4 is extremely important to the students' ability to use a dictionary effortlessly. At first glance, a dictionary entry, especially the phonetic spelling, may seem Greek to your students. This unit will take the *mystery* out of dictionary entries and replace it with *mastery*.

Bulletin Board
Petal Peddler

OBJECTIVE The students will complete dictionary entries correctly.

DESCRIPTION The students choose the missing dictionary entry parts and slip them into place. The back of each flower is an answer key.

SUGGESTIONS FOR USE Use this bulletin board to introduce, review, or reinforce the objective.

MATERIALS
- seed catalogue or other source of flower pictures
- scissors
- tagboard
- white glue
- stapler
- dictionary
- marker

PROCEDURE

1. Cut out as many large flowers as you want to use. Reinforce each flower by gluing it onto tagboard.

2. Cut out a flowerpot for each flower.

3. Find the dictionary entry for each flower and write the definition portion of the entry on the appropriate pot, leaving room for the missing parts of the entry.

4. Staple the flower pots in position on the bulletin board. As you staple, leave a space in the top edge of each pot to slip its flower into.

5. Cut 1-inch-wide strips of tagboard and staple them onto the flowerpots to hold the missing entry parts.

6. Cut 2-inch-wide strips of tagboard and write the missing entry parts on them.

7. Make a pocket to hold the missing entry parts. Fold an 8½-by-11-inch piece of construction paper almost in half and staple it along the edges. Staple the pocket in position on the bulletin board.

8. Write the appropriate answer key on the back of each flower. Slip each flower into its pot.

9. Write the following directions on a piece of construction paper and staple it in position on the bulletin board:

Can You Help the Petal Peddler?

1. Take the missing dictionary entry parts from the pocket.
2. Slide them into the correct places on each pot.
3. Read the key on the back of each flower to check your answers.
4. Return the cards to the pocket.

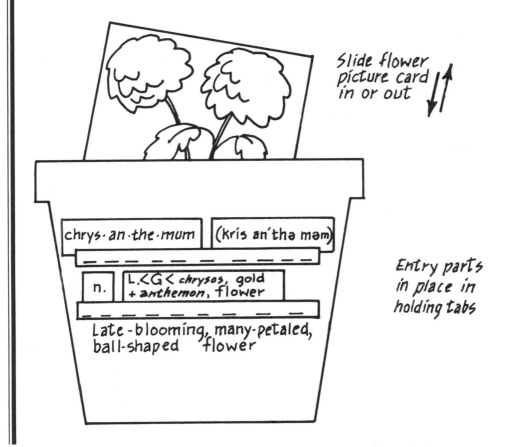

Slide flower picture card in or out

chrys·an·the·mum   (kris an'tha məm)

n.   L.<G< *chrysos*, gold + *anthemon*, flower

Late-blooming, many-petaled, ball-shaped flower

Entry parts in place in holding tabs

Games
Dictionary Entry Puzzle

OBJECTIVE The students will become familiar with the parts of a dictionary entry.

DESCRIPTION The students work as a group to complete dictionary entry puzzles.

bale (bāl) n. a large bundle of tightly packed cotton, hay, straw, etc., wrapped for shipping —V. to make into bales [to bale hay]. -baled, baling

SUGGESTIONS FOR USE Use this low-key game to introduce the dictionary entry to your group. Increase the level of difficulty by placing the pieces for two dictionary entries in the hat at one time. Use this game to review vocabulary from other parts of your curriculum.

MATERIALS
- tagboard, various sizes
- scissors
- marker
- Diction Harry's hat
- dictionary
- rubber bands

PROCEDURE
1. Choose the vocabulary words you wish to use.
2. Write the dictionary entry for one vocabulary word on each piece of tagboard. Cut each entry into its parts and secure the parts with a rubber band for storage.
3. Prepare for the first game by placing the puzzle pieces of one vocabulary word (without the rubber band) in Diction Harry's hat.

4. Explain the rules of the game to your group:
   a. The object is to put the pieces of a dictionary entry in their correct order.
   b. All the pieces are in Diction Harry's hat.
   c. Students will be chosen to draw the puzzle pieces from the hat until all the pieces are gone.
   d. The leader will ask, "Who has the first puzzle piece? Place it in the puzzle correctly."
   e. The leader will continue until the puzzle is complete.
   f. Each player who places a puzzle piece correctly may choose a new player for the next game.

Hold Up!

OBJECTIVE The students will practice finding a word quickly and will use the parts of its dictionary entry.

DESCRIPTION Students compete individually to answer questions about specific dictionary entries, holding up the answer as it is located.

SUGGESTIONS FOR USE Use this busy game when your group needs to let off steam constructively. Minimize the competitive aspect. This game can be adapted to any curriculum area and is especially suited to identification of parts of speech. Check your classroom dictionary to verify the answers.

MATERIALS
- four or more pieces of tagboard, at least 6 inches by 8 inches each
- felt-tip pen
- Diction Harry's hat
- dictionary for each player
- three answer cards, numbered *1, 2,* and *3,* for each player
- paper and pencil for each player

PROCEDURE
1. Prepare the game cards by printing a group of three words on each piece of tagboard. Provide a copy of the matching questions for the game leader. (See the word lists and game questions below.)
2. Place the game cards in Diction Harry's hat.
3. Give a dictionary and a set of answer cards to each player.
4. Give each player a piece of paper and a pencil for keeping a personal score.
5. Explain the rules of the game:
   a. The object is to be the first to hold up the card with the number that tells which word answers the question. There may be two numbers to hold up.
   b. The game cards will be put in the hat.

c. A student will be chosen to draw the first game card and read the three answer words.

d. The leader will read the first question for the game card that was drawn.

e. At the leader's signal, players may open their dictionaries to find the answer.

f. When the answer is found, hold up the number that matches the answer word.

g. The leader will call on the first player who held up a card to give the answer.

h. If the first player is incorrect, the leader will proceed to the second, and so on. The first player who answers correctly gets to choose the next card.

i. Return the card to the hat, discarding a card when all of its questions have been asked.

j. Score one point, on the honor system, for each correct answer you hold up.

WORD LISTS AND QUESTIONS (answers in bold)

A.
1. psalm
2. prepare
3. phoebe

1. Which words are nouns? **psalm, phoebe**
2. Which word begins with an "s" sound? **psalm**
3. Which word has the most derivations? **prepare** (Derivations are new words formed by adding prefixes or suffixes to a root word.)

B.
1. caste
2. calk
3. cell

1. Which word has a short a? **caste**
2. Which word has two spellings? **calk**
3. Which word can be used as a noun or a verb? **calk**

C.
1. forte
2. foyer
3. forsake

1. Which words have more than one pronunciation? **forte, foyer**
2. Which word comes from French? **foyer**
3. Which word has a past tense given? **forsake**

D.
1. Scotsman
2. scout
3. scroll

1. Which word has more than one entry? **scout**
2. Which word has an illustration? **scroll**
3. Which word has the plural given? **Scotsman**

Understanding Dictionary Entries Pretest

A. Put a check beside each item below that you would find listed in a dictionary.

___ 1. D

___ 2. SOS

___ 3. -able

___ 4. r.p.m.

___ 5. hotbed

___ 6. telephotography

___ 7. John Glenn

___ 8. mud puppy

___ 9. im-

___ 10. June bug

B. Read the dictionary entry below. Then answer the questions.

deny /di 'nī/ *vb* **de·nied; de·ny·ing** **1:** to declare not to be true: CONTRADICT (*deny* a report) **2:** to refuse to grant (*deny* a request) **3:** to refuse to acknowledge: DISOWN

1. Does this word rhyme with *angry*? _____

2. Which syllable is accented? _____

3. What part of speech is *deny*? _____

4. How many meanings are given for *deny*? _____

5. Write a synonym for *deny*. _____

Dictionary Entries Match Game

A. Match each entry below with a name. Write the letter of the name in the blank *before* the entry. Then find each entry in your dictionary. Write its page number in the blank *after* the entry.

___ 1. re- p. _____   A. prefix

___ 2. pl. p. _____   B. suffix

___ 3. TNT p. _____   C. compound word written as one word

___ 4. brace p. _____   D. compound written as two words

___ 5. jet engine p. _____   E. compound with a hyphen

___ 6. jet-propelled p. _____   F. abbreviation

___ 7. -ment p. _____   G. single word

___ 8. v p. _____   H. single-letter entry

___ 9. eardrum p. _____   I. capital-letter combination

___ 10. April fool p. _____   J. proper-noun entry

B. Look in your dictionary for some *phrases* that are entries. Write the ones you find. *Example:* coat of arms

_____   _____

_____   _____

_____   _____

Under the Microscope

You need a mental microscope to see all the parts of a dictionary entry. Read the dictionary entry below.

Entry word	Pronunciation (or sound spelling)	Abbreviation for the part of speech

bard /bärd/ *n* in olden times, a poet — Definition
and singer who composed songs about
heroes (Shakespeare is a famous *bard*.) — How the word is used

A. Name the parts of the entry below.

1.	2.	3.

husk /həsk/ *n* the outer covering of a fruit

or seed, as of coconuts or corn 4.

—*v* to strip the husk from, as to *husk* corn

5.	6.

B. Write a dictionary entry for <u>skinny</u>. Then check your work by finding the entry for <u>skinny</u> in the dictionary.

_____

_____

_____

C. Words we use a lot often have very long entries. Which of the words below do you think have long entries? Circle them. Then check your guesses in the dictionary.

1. go   2. skyscraper   3. put

NAME _____

More Under the Microscope

Focus your microscope on the dictionary entry for <u>funny</u> below.

fun·ny /ˈfən ē/ *adj* **fun·ni·er; fun·ni·est 1:** Causing

laughter (a *funny* picture) **2:** strange (a *funny* noise)

A. Below are the names for the parts of a basic dictionary entry. Read the list. Then find, circle, and neatly number each of the parts in the dictionary entry above.

1. main entry word
2. part of speech
3. second definition
4. pronunciation, or sound spelling

5. how the word is used
6. inflected form(s)
7. first definition
8. syllable divider

B. Answer these questions about the dictionary entry for <u>funny</u>.

1. What does the first word tell you? _____

_____

2. What does the word in / ___ / tell you? _____

_____

3. What follows the word in / ___ / ? _____

4. What three other things does the entry tell you?

    a. _____

    b. _____

    c. _____

C. Write your own dictionary entry for <u>happy</u> below. Include all the parts of an entry. Then check your work in the dictionary.

_____

_____

_____

Webster's Assistant

A. Noah Webster was America's first lexicographer
(/lek sə 'käg rə fər/), or dictionary maker. He published the first
dictionary of American English in 1806. He helped the United States
become a strong country by unifying the language of the new nation.

Noah Webster had many new words to add to the first American
dictionary. These were words used in the United States but not in
England. Pretend you are Noah Webster and write a dictionary entry for
each word listed below.

1. applesauce _____

_____

_____

2. moccasin _____

_____

_____

3. skunk _____

_____

_____

4. Why do you think these words were new to the English

language? _____

_____

B. A modern lexicographer also faces Noah Webster's problem of a
constantly changing vocabulary. Check your dictionary. Does it tell you
that BASIC is the name of a special type of computer language? Can
you think of any new words that need to be added to your dictionary?

Write them here. _____

_____

Diction Harry reproducible page, copyright © 1983

Understanding Dictionary Entries Mastery Test

A. Unscramble the dictionary entry below. Copy it neatly in the correct order on the lines below.

/'stäp līt/   **2:** a signal light used in controlling traffic
stop·light 1: a light on the rear of a motor vehicle that lights when the driver uses the brake pedal *n*

_____

_____

_____

B. Read each statement carefully. Write *true* or *false* in the blank in front of each statement.

_____ 1. A dictionary entry tells you how to spell a word.

_____ 2. A dictionary entry may be a single letter.

_____ 3. Benjamin Franklin would be a dictionary entry.

_____ 4. A dictionary entry tells you the meaning of a word.

_____ 5. A dictionary does *not* tell you how to use a word correctly.

_____ 6. A dictionary entry tells you how to say the word.

_____ 7. Easy words do not have meanings.

_____ 8. The dictionary entry shows the syllables of a word.

_____ 9. Many abbreviations are listed as dictionary entries.

_____ 10. In a dictionary entry, *v* or *vb* means ''verb.''

Unit 5

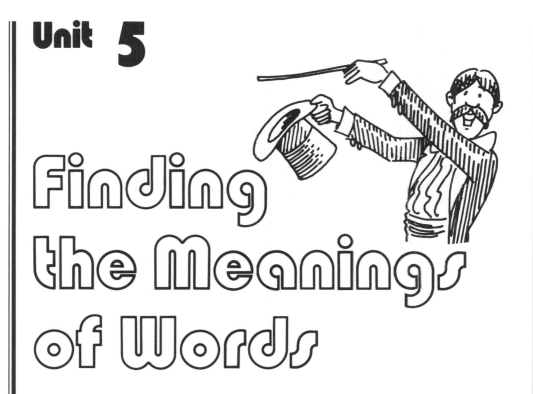

Finding the Meanings of Words

Objective

The students will use the meaning function of a dictionary entry.

Before You Begin

Administer the pretest to determine your students' current skills. Determining the appropriate definition of a given word depends on the context of the word: Students who do poorly on the pretest may need a review of using context to determine meaning. Continue to emphasize the use of guide words in finding entries quickly.

Bulletin Board
The Meaning Machine

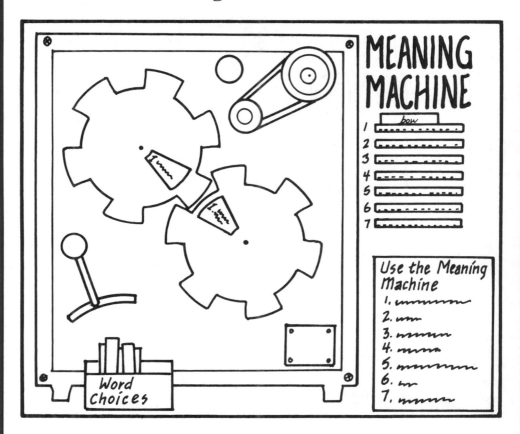

OBJECTIVE The student will match a given homograph with two of its meanings. (A *homograph* is a word that is spelled the same as another word but has a different meaning and usually a different etymology.)

DESCRIPTION The gears turn, revealing the hidden meanings. Of course, the real meaning machine is the dictionary!

SUGGESTIONS FOR USE This bulletin board is a good motivator for using the dictionary to find meanings.

MATERIALS
- heavy plain paper plates or tagboard
- utility knife
- two 1½- to 2-inch brads
- tagboard
- dictionary
- construction paper
- felt-tip pen

PROCEDURE

1. Make the Meaning Machine, except for the gears, from construction paper. Include details, such as buttons or switches. Staple the machine in position on the bulletin board.

2. Cut two congruent circles from tagboard for the gears. (A round trash can is a handy circle pattern.)

3. Divide each gear into 12 equal parts, and cut six 1½-inch-deep teeth in each gear, as in Figure 1.

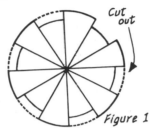

Figure 1

4. Cut one window in each gear, as in Figure 2.

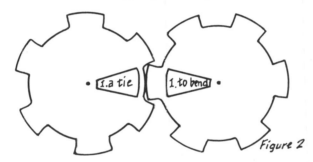

Figure 2

5. Cut out two more circles from tagboard, making them 3 inches smaller in diameter than the gears. These are the meaning circles.

6. Make a list of twelve homographs and two meanings for each homograph. (See the list of suggested homographs on the next page.) Cut twelve tagboard word cards and print one homograph on each card.

7. Place each gear on top of a meaning circle. Fasten the gears on top of the meaning circles with brads. Staple the meaning circles to the board so that the gears interlock and can be turned freely.

8. Print one meaning of the first homograph inside the window on the second gear. Print the second meaning inside the window on the second gear.

9. Turn one gear until the next tooth of one gear fits in the next notch of the other. Write meanings for the second homographs inside the windows. Continue turning the gears and writing in meanings until you have come back to the first meanings.

10. Make a pocket from a piece of 8½-by-11-inch construction paper. Fold the paper almost in half and staple along the edges. Label the pocket Word Cards. Staple the pocket in position on the bulletin board, and place the word cards in it.

11. Cut twelve 1-by-10-inch strips of tagboard as holding strips for the word cards. Staple them along the bottom and number them.

12. Prepare the caption and staple it in position on the bulletin board.

13. Provide a dictionary for the students to use to check answers.

14. Print the following directions on a piece of construction paper:

Use the Meaning Machine

1. Take the word cards from the pocket.
2. Place a word card in the Word Slot.
3. Turn the top gear until you find a meaning for the word.
4. The bottom gear will automatically turn to show another meaning for the word.
5. Find the dictionary entry for the word and check your machine "output." The dictionary is the real meaning machine!
6. Do steps 2 through 5 for each word.
7. Return the word cards to the pocket when you are finished.

HOMOGRAPH LIST

Homograph	Meanings
bow	forward part of a ship; bend
fair	market; beautiful
run	move fast; score in baseball
train	practice; group of railway cars
can	container; know how to
grub	dig up; food
contract	legal agreement; get smaller
conduct	behavior; lead
row	orderly group of things; move a boat with oars
tear	rip; drop of liquid from the eye
entrance	opening; fill with wonder
present	display; being at hand

Game

OBJECTIVE The students will use their dictionaries to find words that fit given meanings.

DESCRIPTION Each player races to find the word that matches the given meaning.

SUGGESTIONS FOR USE Reinforce the value of using guide words to locate entries quickly. Use this game to introduce the meaning portion of the entry. Use your own list of vocabulary words you wish to introduce to your group.

MATERIALS

- Diction Harry's magic hat and wand
- dictionary for each player

- tagboard
- felt-tip pen
- chalkboard
- chalk

PROCEDURE

1. Prepare the meaning cards and a matching list of words for guesses. (See the list of suggestions below.)

2. Place the meaning cards in the hat.

3. Provide a dictionary for each player.

4. Explain the rules to your group:

    a. The object of Guess Again! is to be the first to find the word that matches the meaning on the meaning card.

    b. A card will be drawn from the hat.

    c. The meaning will be read aloud.

    d. Three words for guessing will be written on the chalkboard.

    e. When the leader says "Go!" choose one of the guesses and find it in your dictionary.

    f. Read the meanings. If you made the right guess, raise your hand. If not, "Guess Again!"

    g. When everyone has found the correct word, the first player who found it will read the word and then its meaning to prove the correct word was located. If the first player is incorrect, the second player will be called on, and so on.

    h. The first player with the correct answer gets to choose the next card.

MEANINGS AND WORD GUESSES LISTS (answers in bold)

Meanings	Guesses
a. **1:** sleeping **2:** as if asleep; quiet **3:** inactive, as some animals or plants in winter	a. composite fusion **dormant**
b. **1:** to plunge into water **2:** to put out	b. **douse** shackle nebula
c. **1:** ten thousand **2:** an indefinitely large number	c. naive **myriad** botany
d. rounded like a ball or the outside of a circle	d. probe gyrate **convex**
e. **1:** the orderly universe **2:** a tall garden plant related to daisies	e. **cosmos** recluse haggard
f. **1:** a log or plank for supporting something on the ground **2:** a runner on which an airplane or helicopter lands **3:** to slide	f. laurel diadem **skid**
g. a rain cloud of uniform grayness that extends over the whole sky	g. levee **nimbus** parsnip

Finding the Meanings of Words Pretest

A. Read these meanings for the word <u>can</u>.

a. know how to
b. be mentally or physically able to
c. have permission to
d. container, usually in the shape of a cylinder
e. contents of a can
f. put in a can; preserve by sealing

Read each sentence below. Decide which of the above meanings of <u>can</u> fits the sentence. Write the number of the meaning in the blank.

____ 1. She <u>can</u> read a road map.

____ 2. Does she <u>can</u> vegetables?

____ 3. She <u>can</u> lift 50 kilograms.

____ 4. She will empty the garbage <u>can</u>.

____ 5. She <u>can</u> go swimming with us.

____ 6. <u>Can</u> she swim the crawl?

____ 7. Is there a <u>can</u> of vegetable soup for lunch?

B. Circle the correct meaning for the underlined word in each sentence below.

1. Are you ready to start a new <u>project</u>?   plan *or* stick out

2. A jet can <u>cruise</u> at 750 km/h.   travel *or* trip

3. Jack needed one more coin to complete the <u>set</u>.   group *or* place

It All Depends...

A. The meaning you choose from the ones given in your dictionary depends on how a word is used in a sentence, that is, the *context* of the word. Find the entries for <u>bow</u> in your dictionary. Write the meaning that explains how <u>bow</u> is used in each sentence.

1. An Indian would use a <u>bow</u> for hunting.

   _____

2. When you meet the Queen of England you might <u>bow</u> to her.

   _____

3. I fished from the <u>bow</u> of the rowboat.

   _____

4. The girl wore a <u>bow</u> in her hair.

   _____

B. Read each sentence below. Find each underlined word in your dictionary. Write the definition for each word that fits the context of the sentence.

1. A magician can <u>palm</u> a card.

   _____

2. The <u>slight</u> girl was very strong for her size.

   _____

3. The baby liked to play with the brightly colored <u>blocks</u>.

   _____

4. The backyard was very <u>level</u>.

   _____

Which Witch Is Which?

A. Find the meaning of each underlined word. Then decide if the sentence is *true* or *false*, and tell why.

1. The <u>wicked</u> witch wanted to hurt the beautiful princess. <u>True.</u>
   <u>Wicked means dangerous, vile.</u>

2. A witch uses a broom for a <u>transport</u>. _____

   _____

3. A witch would live in a <u>plover</u>. _____

   _____

4. A witch's clothing would be <u>somber</u>. _____

   _____

B. The definition section of a dictionary will also help you find *synonyms*. Sometimes the synonyms are listed in a part of the entry called *syn*. Synonyms may also be printed in capital letters. Find a synonym for each word below. Use your dictionary.

1. good _____   6. pretty _____

2. give _____   7. give _____

3. bad _____   8. baffle _____

4. wily _____   9. lurk _____

5. power _____   10. cold _____

C. *Homographs* are different words with the same spelling. They are listed more than once in your dictionary. Find <u>box</u> in your dictionary. Write three meanings for <u>box</u>.

1. _____

2. _____

3. _____

D. Extra for Experts: Find three homographs with three or more entries. Write them below.

1. _____   2. _____   3. _____

Picture Riddles

Use your dictionary to solve the riddles below. For each riddle, write the word in the first blank and the letter of the picture in the second blank.

Riddle	Word	Picture
1. I have a pouch like a kangaroo. I like to burrow.	plaid	a.
_____ __		
2. A pattern. If you are a Scot, your clan has one.	nosegay	b.
_____ __		
3. It produces seeds.	sloop	c.
_____ __		
4. A small bouquet	wombat	d.
_____ __		
5. A type of hat	ketch	e.
_____ __		
6. Smaller than a greyhound	whippet	f.
_____ __		
7. I have one mast.	derby	g.
_____ __		
8. I have two masts.	pistil	h.
_____ __		

Substitutions

A. A good writer tries to avoid using overworked words. Read the dictionary entry for each word listed below. Write two synonyms you could substitute for each word to make your writing more interesting.

1. know _____ _____

2. terrible _____ _____

3. real _____ _____

4. quiet _____ _____

5. say _____ _____

6. easy _____ _____

B. Use your dictionary to find a more vivid substitute for each underlined word below. Then rewrite the sentence to make it more interesting.

1. John liked to <u>talk</u> all day about his motorbike.

_____

2. The sunset was <u>pretty</u>. _____

3. Boy, was I <u>surprised</u>! _____

4. Did you see how <u>fast</u> that dog <u>ate</u> his dinner?

_____

C. Extra for Experts: Unscramble the letters to find the words that fit the meanings. Each word begins with <u>g</u>. You may use your dictionary.

Meaning	Scramble	Word
1. craft, cunning	giuel	_____
2. small fish	gdeugno	_____
3. distort the meaning	grebla	_____
4. gaudy	ghrias	_____

Diction Harry reproducible page, copyright © 1983

Finding the Meanings of Words Mastery Test

A. Find the dictionary entries for <u>still</u>. Write the definition of <u>still</u> that fits each sentence below.

1. The city is very <u>still</u> at night. _____

2. The water in our pond is <u>still</u>. _____

3. He <u>still</u> believes in magic. _____

B. Use your dictionary to write one definition for each word below.

1. fret _____

2. idle _____

3. condense _____

4. ecstasy _____

5. anticipate _____

6. quill _____

C. Write three definitions for each homograph below. Use your dictionary.

1. chase

_____

_____

_____

2. seal

_____

_____

_____

Unit 6

Syllables, Accents, and Spellings

Objective

The students will use their dictionaries to determine correct syllabications, accents, and spellings.

Before You Begin

Use the pretest to determine the needs of individual students. Present those activities that are indicated.

Bulletin Boards
Divide the Treasure

OBJECTIVE The students will use a dictionary to find correct syllabications of words.

DESCRIPTION The student moves pointers to show the syllabication of a given word and then uses the dictionary to check the divisions.

SUGGESTIONS FOR USE Use this bulletin board at any time during this unit. Also use it in conjunction with a review of syllable rules.

MATERIALS
- tagboard
- sentence strips
- felt-tip pen
- utility knife
- stapler

PROCEDURE

1. Cut four treasure chests out of tagboard. Make a pair of slits in three of the treasure chests to hold word cards. The fourth chest holds the directions. Staple the chests in position on the bulletin board.

2. Print treasure words on the sentence strips. (See the suggestions for treasure words below.)

3. Cut 1½-inch-wide strips from the tagboard. The length must match that of the treasure chests.

4. Make three pointers, at least 5 inches high, for each chest. Cut slits in the pointers and slide three pointers on each strip.

5. Staple the pointer strips in position on the bulletin board. Be sure the pointers can slide.

6. Prepare the caption and staple it in position on the bulletin board.

7. Print the following directions on the fourth treasure chest:

Divide the Treasure

1. Slide the pointers to show where each treasure word should be divided into syllables.
2. Use the dictionary to check your answers.
3. Move the pointers to the right when you are finished.

TREASURE WORDS LIST onyx, opalescent, diamond, pendant, bracelet, emerald, jewelry, sapphire, diadem

Blotto

OBJECTIVE The students will use a dictionary to find correct spellings for words.

DESCRIPTION Balloons with cutouts are positioned to reveal the correct spellings. The students check their choices with the dictionary.

SUGGESTIONS FOR USE Blotto is appropriate for any vocabulary development goal. The balloons may be changed easily to update the bulletin board to your current curriculum needs.

MATERIALS
- overhead projector
- transparency
- pen
- scissors
- hole punch
- pushpins
- yarn
- stapler
- dictionary

PROCEDURE

1. Make Blotto, the clown. Trace him on a transparency and use the overhead projector to scale his size to fit your bulletin board space.

2. The size of your bulletin board will determine how many balloons you need to make. Make a balloon pattern and then cut out two balloons for each balloon space.

3. Using one balloon for each space, print groups of three words, two of which are misspelled in each group. Use words that suit the vocabulary needs of your group.

4. For each word balloon, make an answer balloon. Cut out a window that matches the position of the correctly spelled word.

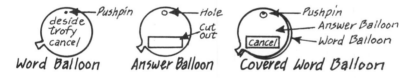

5. Position the word balloons, cut the appropriate lengths of yarn, and staple these items to the bulletin board.

6. Position a pushpin on each word balloon to hold the answer balloons.

7. Use a hole punch to make a hole in each answer balloon. Each hole must line up with the appropriate pushpin.

8. Make a pocket for the answer balloons. Fold a piece of 8½-by-11-inch paper almost in half and staple along the edges. Label the pocket Blotto's Balloon Bank. Staple the pocket in position on the bulletin board.

9. Supply a dictionary for checking answers.

10. Prepare the caption and staple it in position on the bulletin board.

11. Print the following directions on a piece of paper and staple it in position on the bulletin board:

Blotto

1. Help Blotto find the correctly spelled words.
2. Take the answer balloons out of the balloon bank.

3. Find the answer balloon that will let the correctly spelled word on each word balloon show through. Hang the answer balloons up.
4. Check your answers with the dictionary.
5. Return the answer balloons to the bank when you are finished.

Game
Break an Egg

OBJECTIVE The students will use the syllable part of dictionary entries.

DESCRIPTION Riddles are used to introduce the syllable part of a dictionary entry. Competition is minimal.

SUGGESTIONS FOR USE Use this activity to introduce and motivate your group as they begin Unit 6.

MATERIALS
- Diction Harry's magic hat and wand
- three plastic eggs (empty stocking containers)
- slips of paper
- 3-by-5-inch index cards
- felt-tip pen
- dictionary for each player

PROCEDURE
1. Print the riddles on the slips of paper and the corresponding answers on the index cards. (See the list of suggestions below.)
2. Place riddle number 1 in an egg and put the egg and its answer card in the hat.
3. Explain the rules to your group:
    a. The goal is to answer the riddle correctly.
    b. The magic wand will be waved and an egg will be pulled from the hat.
    c. The riddle inside the egg will be read aloud.
    d. Whoever answers the riddle correctly according to the dictionary will break the next egg.

RIDDLE WORDS LIST
1. When is it impossible to break an egg?
When <u>egg</u> is a dictionary entry!
2. When is it possible to break a lightbulb?
When <u>light•bulb</u> is a dictionary entry!
3. When can you break a window and not get in trouble?
When <u>win•dow</u> is a dictionary entry!
4. Some other riddle words are <u>leg</u>, <u>ankle</u>, and <u>silence</u>.

Syllables, Accents, and Spellings Pretest

A. Read each statement below. Write *true* or *false* in the blank next to each statement.

_____ 1. The dictionary shows the syllables of a word.

_____ 2. Knowing where a word is divided into syllables will help you pronounce it.

_____ 3. Accent marks are used to show which syllables are stressed.

_____ 4. Some words may have more than one accented syllable.

_____ 5. The stronger accent mark is called the *secondary* accent.

_____ 6. When you are writing, you should use the dictionary to check the spelling of each word.

B. Circle the accented syllable or syllables in each word below.

1. 'di al

2. 'prob a bly

3. re 'gret ta ble

4. ex cla 'ma tion

C. There is one correctly spelled plural in each row below. Circle each correct spelling.

1. monkies	monkeys	monkeies
2. ranchs	ranchies	ranches
3. glasses	glassies	glass's
4. spies	spyes	spys
5. boxs	boxes	boxies

Be SAS·sy: Know Syllables, Accents, and Spellings!

A. How does your dictionary show syllables? Find the word <u>volcano</u> in your dictionary. Below, put a check next to the pattern your dictionary uses to show syllables.

___ 1. Syllables shown by spaces: vol ca no

___ 2. Syllables shown by dots: vol•ca•no

___ 3. Syllables shown in the phonetic spelling: volcano (väl ′kā nō)

B. The *accent* is a mark that shows which syllable is stressed. How does your dictionary show accented syllables? Find the word <u>lava</u> in your dictionary and look at the phonetic spelling. Below, put a check next to the pattern your dictionary uses.

___ 1. In front of the stressed syllable: ′lä və

___ 2. After the stressed syllable: lä′ və

C. Circle the accent mark below that your dictionary uses.

ı   ′

D. Using your dictionary's pattern, write the syllables and the accents for each word below. Read the definitions, too.

1. mountain _____   4. magma _____

2. volcanic _____   5. atmosphere _____

3. geology _____   6. cone _____

E. Extra for Experts: Read the paragraph below. Find the correct spelling for each underlined word and write it below.

Mt. St. Helens was a <u>dorment</u> volcano in the Cascades until March 28, 1980. Geologists were very interested in this first <u>aruption</u> on the United States mainland in 63 years. The blasts from Mt. St. Helens <u>devestated</u> 200 square miles of the state of Washington. Scientists are still <u>monotoring</u> this volcano.

_____   _____   _____   _____

NAME _____

Picture It!

A. A dictionary can help you find the correct spelling of a word. Read each sentence below. Use the pictures as clues to the missing words. Check your dictionary for the correct spellings and then fill in the blanks.

1. The _____ collects nuts for its winter food supply.

2. The _____ is much larger than a monkey.

3. For safety, soft drinks are sold in

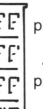

plastic _____.

4. A baseball _____ must practice every day.

5. The office _____ had four floors.

6. We grew corn, tomatoes, and squash

in our _____ garden.

7. We had slices of _____ at the picnic.

8. Jane always wears a helmet when she

rides her _____.

B. A dictionary will help you spell unusual plurals. Do you remember that *pl* means plural? Use your dictionary to find the plurals of the words below. Write the plurals.

1. goose _____   5. mother-in-law _____

2. mosquito _____   6. piccolo _____

3. journey _____   7. sheep _____

4. hoof _____   8. jalopy _____

Flying High or Low

A. Look up each word below in your dictionary. Use your dictionary's pattern to show the syllables and accents of each word. Also tell on which page you found the word in your dictionary.

Word	Syllables & Accents	Page
1. engine	_____	_____
2. piston	_____	_____
3. rudder	_____	_____
4. pilot	_____	_____
5. hangar	_____	_____
6. propeller	_____	_____

B. Some words have more than one accented syllable. The heavy accent is called the *primary* accent. The lighter accent is called the *secondary* accent. The secondary accent may be shown with a low mark or with a lighter high mark. Find your dictionary's pattern for showing primary and secondary accents by locating the entry for locomotive. Copy the part of the entry for locomotive that shows the primary and secondary accents.

_____

C. Syllabicate and accent each word below. Use your dictionary.

1. engineer	_____	4. caboose	_____
2. roundhouse	_____	5. ticket	_____
3. conductor	_____	6. controller	_____

D. Some words have two primary accents. Syllabicate and accent each word below. Circle each word that has two primary accents. Use your dictionary.

1. airline	_____	4. airtight	_____
2. airplane	_____	5. airmail	_____
3. airstrip	_____	6. airport	_____

Write it Right!

A. Use your dictionary to find the correct spellings of the words listed below. Circle the correct spelling in each row.

1. seperate	sepparate	separate
2. beutiful	beautiful	beautifull
3. excellent	excellant	exellent
4. cannoe	cannu	canoe
5. athaletic	atheletic	athletic
6. sissors	scissers	scissors

B. *Inflections* are changes you have to make in the spelling of noun words in order to form the possessive or plural and in the spelling of verbs in order to form the past tense or third person singular present indicative. The dictionary will tell you how to spell unusual or confusing inflected forms. Word forms in which you simply add **-s, -es, -ed,** or **-ing** without changing the internal spelling of the word are usually *not* shown. Use your dictionary to write the inflected forms of each word below. Use the entry marked *v* for "verb" to find them.

1. picnic _____

2. seek _____

3. swim _____

4. dive _____

5. ski _____

C. Your dictionary will help you find the correct spellings of unusual comparative and superlative forms for adjectives and adverbs. If there is no listing, assume you add -*er* and -*est*. With longer adjectives and adverbs, *more* and *most* are used. Use your dictionary to find the correct spellings of the comparative and superlative forms of each word below.

1. bad _____   _____

2. dense _____   _____

3. comely _____   _____

Syllables, Accents, and Spellings Mastery Test

A. Read each statement and decide which are true and which are false. Write *true* or *false* in each blank.

_____ 1. The primary accent is the stronger or strongest.

_____ 2. All two-syllable words have a secondary accent.

_____ 3. There may be more than one correct way to make a word plural.

_____ 4. You should use your dictionary to check the spelling of *every* word.

_____ 5. The dictionary will help you spell unusual or confusing inflected forms.

_____ 6. When two spellings for the same word are listed, only the first one is right.

B. Rewrite each word below showing the syllabication and accents.

1. arduous _____

2. bazaar _____

3. confirmation _____

4. entertainer _____

C. Use your dictionary to find the plural of each word below.

1. money _____

2. jack-of-all-trades _____

3. trout _____

4. trustee _____

5. phenomenon _____

Unit 7

Using the Pronunciation Key

Objective

The students will use a pronunciation key as an aid to correct pronunciation.

Before You Begin

Administer the pretest to determine your students' current level of skills. Using a pronunciation key effectively is a difficult skill. Monitor your students' progress and review as necessary.

Note Pronunciation keys vary from dictionary to dictionary. We have used the pronunciation symbols found in the Webster's New Elementary Dictionary. Although most of these materials require the student to use the pronunciation key found in a classroom dictionary, being able to interpret different keys is a most useful skill, and your students should have little difficulty changing gears when necessary.

Bulletin Board
Drȯ T͟hēz, Plēz

OBJECTIVE The students will follow directions written phonetically.

DESCRIPTION Behind each door is a mystery direction telling the student to draw or write something.

SUGGESTIONS FOR USE The lure of the unknown will make this bulletin board popular with your students. Change the mystery directions and answer key to maintain interest.

MATERIALS
- laminated paper *or* plain drawing paper
- wipe-off crayons
- overhead projector
- transparency
- pen
- writing surface at the bulletin board
- construction paper
- stapler

PROCEDURE

1. Make Diction Harry the artist. Use the overhead projector and a transparency to copy him. Staple him in position on the bulletin board.

2. Prepare a drawing surface. Laminate, or cover with plastic, two 8½-by-11-inch pieces of white paper. (As an alternative, supply sheets of drawing paper for each student.) Place the drawing surfaces and crayons at the bulletin board. Supply wipe-off materials if needed.

3. Make the doors: Number four sheets of 8½-by-11-inch construction paper from 1 through 4. Label a fifth sheet Lift fȯr Kē.

4. Print one of the following instructions on each of four matching sheets of construction paper:

   a. Door 1: Drȯ thrē skwaərz, ēch wi<u>th</u> fīv-inch sīdz.

   b. Door 2: Rīt yər nām in <u>th</u>ə fərst skwaər.

   c. Door 3: Drȯ yər 'fa və rət füd in <u>th</u>ə 'sek ənd wən.

   d. Door 4: Rīt <u>th</u>ə nām əv yər lēst 'fa və rət spōrt in <u>th</u>ə thərd wən.

5. On a fifth piece of matching construction paper, print an answer key that tells what the mystery directions actually say.

6. Staple the instruction sheets and answer sheet in position on the bulletin board. Cover these with the appropriately labeled doors. Staple the doors along the top edges only.

7. Prepare the caption and position it on the bulletin board.

8. Print the following directions, adjusted for the drawing materials you have chosen, on a piece of construction paper:

Drȯ <u>Th</u>ēz, Plēz

   1. Take a crayon and a piece of drawing paper.
   2. Open door 1 and follow the mystery direction.
   3. Then follow the mystery directions behind doors 2, 3, and 4 in order.
   4. Open the answer door and check your drawings.
   5. Clean up the work area when you are finished.

Games
Caesar's Salve

OBJECTIVE The students will use the phonetic spelling and meaning parts of dictionary entries to unlock confusing sentences.

DESCRIPTION This is a minimal-competition activity in which a confusing group of words is arranged to make a sentence. Students use the dictionary as an aid.

SUGGESTIONS FOR USE Use this activity to introduce the pronunciation key and to stress its importance. It fits best between duplicating masters Using Key Words (page 81) and Fə 'net iks (page 82).

MATERIALS
- Diction Harry's magic hat and wand
- sentence strips
- felt-tip pen
- scissors
- dictionary for each player

PROCEDURE
1. Print a confusing sentence on sentence strips and cut the sentence apart into individual words. (See the list of suggestions below.)
2. Put the words for a sentence into the hat.
3. Explain the following rules to your group:
    a. The goal is to make a sentence using the words in the hat and then interpret its meaning.
    b. A student will be chosen to wave the magic wand and pick a word card.
    c. The leader will say "Go!" and everyone else is to find the dictionary entry for that word.
    d. The first player who raises his or her hand and pronounces and defines the word correctly gets to pick the next word.
    e. When all the words are chosen, the players with the word cards will arrange themselves so that they are in sentence order.

SENTENCE LIST
1. Caesar's salve remedied the peasants' pneumonic malady. (When cutting apart, make *the peasants'* one card.)
2. Caesar's retinue catered to his every caprice. (When cutting apart, make *to his every caprice* one card.)
3. Caesar's centurions condoned the pillaging of the vanquished barbarians. (When cutting apart, make *the pillaging* one card and *of the vanquished* another.)

Rhyming Race

OBJECTIVE The students will use phonetic spellings as an aid in choosing rhyming words for given words.

DESCRIPTION Teams compete to find the most rhyming words for each mystery word.

SUGGESTIONS FOR USE Use this game at any stage in your group's skill development. As cooperation is required among team members, game playing is a healthy way to develop the skill of being a good team member. The rules can be easily adapted to make this a game of individual competition.

MATERIALS
- Diction Harry's magic hat and wand
- sentence strips
- felt-tip pen
- scissors
- dictionary for each player
- piece of paper and pencil for each team

PROCEDURE
1. Print mystery words on sentence strips and cut the strips apart into individual words. (See the list of suggested words below.)
2. Place the words in the magic hat.
3. Divide your group into teams. Have each team pick a recorder. Arrange the teams in circles or at tables. Supply a dictionary for each player.
4. Explain the following rules to the players:
   a. The object of the game is to help your team find and write the longest list of rhyming words in four minutes.
   b. A mystery word for rhyming will be drawn from the magic hat.
   c. The recorder will write the word on the team record sheet.
   d. When the leader says "Go!" find the mystery word in your dictionary and read its pronunciation.
   e. Then begin searching your dictionary for rhyming words.
   f. The recorder will list the rhyming words you find. Words must be spelled correctly.
   g. When time is up, the leader will say "Stop." The scoring is as follows:

> three-letter words—1 point
> four-letter words—2 points
> five-letter words—3 points
> etc.

(If this scoring method seems too cumbersome, score one point for each correct word.) The highest score wins.

WORD LIST
chamois, choir, forte, gnaw, phial, psalm, queue, xylem

Using the Pronunciation Key Pretest

A. Circle the correct phonetic spelling for each word below.

1. sight   /sīght/   /sīt/   /sit/
2. came   /kām/   /came/   /cam/
3. bays   /bās/   /bāys/   /bāz/
4. sitter   /'sit er/   /'sit tər/   /'sit ər/
5. giant   /'jī ənt/   /'gī ant/   /'ji ənt/

B. Study each pronunciation at the left and the words at the right below. Circle the word for which each pronunciation stands.

1. /kāj/   cage   keg   sage   sag
2. /stil/   stile   stole   still   sill
3. /nek/   knack   knee   niece   neck
4. /fōn/   foam   phone   fond   fone
5. /chēk/   check   cheek   cheap   keep

C. Underline the words in each row below that contain the sound represented by each symbol.

1. /ō/   tow   too   show   hoe   boot
2. /k/   cat   sack   chrome   sake   scene
3. /o͞o/   bow   fool   to   blue   knew
4. /j/   gem   give   edge   ginger   jam
5. /s/   sew   was   cinder   single   can

Using Key Words

A. Find the short pronunciation key at the bottom of a page in your dictionary. Write the key word in your dictionary that matches each underlined sound below.

1. sh<u>ou</u>t _____

2. m<u>i</u>tt _____

3. b<u>a</u>se _____

4. play<u>er</u> _____

5. <u>ch</u>eer _____

6. <u>s</u>hortstop _____

7. str<u>i</u>ke _____

8. <u>c</u>atcher _____

9. <u>u</u>mpire _____

10. inni<u>ng</u> _____

B. The *schwa* symbol is one of the most frequently used symbols. The schwa symbol is ə. Say the word *about* to yourself. The sound you hear for the letter *a* is the schwa sound.

Say each word below to yourself. Circle the words that contain a schwa sound. If you are not sure, check your dictionary.

1. silent

2. second

3. steal

4. fielder

5. bunt

6. uniform

7. batter

8. double

9. home run

10. dugout

C. Using your dictionary, write the phonetic spelling of each word listed below. (The phonetic spelling follows the main entry.)

1. cake _____

2. isle _____

3. phone _____

4. though _____

5. ice _____

6. knee _____

7. quart _____

8. gang _____

Diction Harry reproducible page, copyright © 1983

Fə'net iks

A. The phonetic spellings are often called "sound spellings" because they show the *sounds* you *hear*. Find <u>laugh</u> in your dictionary.

1. Copy the phonetic spelling. _____

2. Which vowel is silent in <u>laugh</u>? _____

3. What sound does the <u>gh</u> make? _____

B. The phonetic spelling should always be checked when you are not sure of a word's pronunciation. Find the phonetic spellings of each word below in your dictionary. Copy the phonetic spellings and practice saying the words to yourself.

1. deny _____   5. tongs _____

2. staunch _____   6. clause _____

3. quince _____   7. slosh _____

4. vehicle _____   8. pharynx _____

C. Be a spelling detective. Use your dictionary to find the correct word or words for each phonetic spelling below.

1. /fīt/ _____   4. /thȯt/ _____

2. /drej/ _____   5. /wāt/ _____

3. /mōp/ _____   _____

D. Be a lexicographer! Write the phonetic spelling of each word below. When you are finished, check your answers in your dictionary.

Word	My Phonetic Spelling	Dictionary's Phonetic Spelling
1. city	_____	_____
2. street	_____	_____
3. light	_____	_____
4. apartment	_____	_____

Diction Harry reproducible page, copyright © 1983

Phonetic Jokes

fa**t** **ā**pe **c**ä**r** **t**e**n** **ē**ven **h**i**t** **b**ī**te** **g**ō **h**ȯ**rn** **t**o͞o**l**

boo**k** **c**oi**n** **u**p **s**ing **th**en **s**oú**nd** **ə** = **a** in about

A. Use the pronunciation key to read the joke below. Then write the joke correctly.

boi: hwəts <u>th</u>at string tīd ə 'roúnd yər 'fin gər fȯr?

_____

gərl: to͞o ri 'mīnd mē to͞o māl ə 'let ər.

_____

boi: did yo͞o māl it?

_____

gərl: ī fər 'gät to͞o rīt it!

_____

B. Read this joke. Then write it correctly.

'däk tər: hwət 'hap ənd to͞o yo͞o?

_____

'pā shənt: ī thro͞o ə 'hȯrs sho͞o 'o vər mī 'shōl dər.

_____

'däk tər: sō?

_____

'pā shənt: <u>th</u>aər wəz ə hȯrs nāld to͞o it!

_____

Phonetic Riddles

Read the riddles below. Then write them correctly.

1. Question: hwət did thə tīd sā az it left thə bēch?

   _____

   Answer: 'nəth ing, it jəst wāvd.

   _____

2. Question: hwī did thə 'tē chər waər 'sən glas əz?

   _____

   Answer: bi 'kȯz hər klas wəz sō brīt.

   _____

3. Question: hwət wəz thə 'tert 'l 'dōō ing ȯn thə 'frē wā?

   _____

   Answer: ə 'baut thrē mīlz an 'aȯr.

   _____

4. Question: hwen iz it im 'päs ə b'l tōō bī ə 'tik ət tōō thə mōōn?

   _____

   Answer: hwen thə mōōn iz fool.

   _____

5. Question: if yōō find därth 'vā dər, 'drak yōō lə, 'frang kən stīn, ənd ə wich 'däk tər ȯn yər 'dȯr ˌstep, hwət shood yōō dōō?

   _____

   _____

   Answer: hōp itz hal ə 'wēn.

   _____

Môr Fə´net iks

A. Some words have more than one acceptable pronunciation. Find two phonetic spellings for each word below. Write them and circle the pronunciation you prefer.

1. roof   _____   _____

2. apricot   _____   _____

3. yours   _____   _____

4. paradise   _____   _____

B. Sometimes the written syllables in the main entry and the spoken syllables in the phonetic spelling do not match: fa•vor•ite *and* ´fāv rit

Find the entry for <u>schism</u>.

1. How many syllables does the main entry show? ____

2. How many syllables does the phonetic spelling show? ____

C. Find the entry for each word below. Write *yes* if the spoken and written syllables are the same. Write *no* if the spoken and written syllables do not match.

_____ 1. president   _____ 4. legend

_____ 2. actor   _____ 5. shellac

_____ 3. elephant   _____ 6. hyphen

D. Riddle time! Write this riddle correctly.

Question: hwī wər <u>th</u>ə ´lit ´l ´snē kərz ən ´hap ē?

_____

Answer: <u>th</u>ər ´fä <u>th</u>ər wəz ə ´lō fər.

_____

NAME _____

Using the Pronunciation Key Mastery Test

A. Read each statement below and decide if it is true or false. Write *true* or *false* in the blanks.

_____ 1. The phonetic spelling shows all the sounds you hear when you say a word.

_____ 2. A letter (for example, *e*) has only one sound.

_____ 3. Silent letters are left out of the phonetic spellings.

_____ 4. Every word has one correct pronunciation.

_____ 5. The schwa sound has many correct spellings.

B. Write the pronunciation symbol for the underlined part of each word.

1. <u>c</u>atch _____   6. <u>ph</u>oto _____

2. op<u>e</u>n _____   7. <u>qu</u>ite _____

3. li<u>gh</u>t _____   8. <u>g</u>iant _____

4. wa<u>s</u> _____   9. f<u>la</u>ke _____

5. sl<u>o</u>t _____   10. cla<u>w</u> _____

C. Circle the correct phonetic spelling for each word.

1. drainpipe   /ˈdran pīp/   /ˈdrān pīp/   /ˈdroin pīp/
2. stage   /stāj/   /stāg/   /stag/
3. circle   /ˈcər kəl/   /cir ˈkəl/   /ˈsər kəl/
4. journey   /ˈjər ny/   /ˈjȯr nē/   /ˈjər nē/
5. lots   /lätz/   /läts/   /lāts/

Unit 8

Parts of Speech and Inflected Forms

Objective

The student will use the dictionary to find the part of speech and inflected forms of given words.

Before You Begin

Administer the pretest to determine your students' degree of familiarity with these dictionary functions. This unit will reinforce your grammar lessons and introduce to your students the dictionary as a grammar reference.

Note More advanced dictionaries do not list inflected forms that follow the standard rules for spelling.

Bulletin Boards
Who Laid the Egg?

OBJECTIVE The student will match root words and suffixes.

DESCRIPTION Let your creativity show when you make the imaginary suffix birds for this bulletin board. Their nests hold the root word eggs that match the suffixes.

SUGGESTIONS FOR USE This bulletin board is appropriate any time your group is working with suffixes. You can also change the suffixes to prefixes.

MATERIALS
- overhead projector
- transparency
- pen
- scissors

PROCEDURE

1. Make three suffix birds and four nests. Trace the birds and nests on a transparency and use the overhead projector to enlarge them for your board.

2. Make an egg pattern and cut out a dozen eggs. Print these root words on the eggs: hope, watch, amaze, quick, recognize, adorn, encourage, flavor, slight, probably, peace, sad.

3. Print these suffix labels for the birds: *-ly* Bird, *-ment* Bird, *-ful* Bird.

4. Print Egg Bank on one nest.

5. Staple the birds and nests in position on the board. Staple the nests around the bottom edges only, making a pocket to hold the root word eggs. Put the eggs in the Egg Bank nest.

6. Prepare the caption and staple it in position on the bulletin board.

7. Make an answer key. Fold a piece of 8½-by-11-inch paper in half. On the front, print Answer Key. Lift the flap and print the answers inside. Position the answer key and staple it to the bulletin board.

8. Print the following directions on a piece of 8½-by-11 inch paper:

Who Laid the Egg?

1. Take the root word eggs from the Egg Bank.
2. Match the root word with the correct suffix bird. Put the egg in the bird's nest.
3. Check your answers with the answer key.
4. Return the eggs to the Egg Bank.

The Balancing Act

OBJECTIVE The students will use the dictionary to determine the parts of speech for given words.

DESCRIPTION Seals are on pedestals labeled with parts of speech. Vocabulary words are written on balls for the seals to balance when the student makes the correct matches.

SUGGESTIONS FOR USE Prepare this bulletin board when your students know where to find the part of speech in a dictionary entry.

MATERIALS
- hole punch
- pushpins
- overhead projector
- transparency
- pen
- saucer
- scissors

PROCEDURE

1. Make three seals and three pedestals. Trace a seal and a pedestal on a transparency and use the overhead projector to enlarge them for your board.

2. Make a list of approximately 12 current vocabulary words that will fit any three part-of-speech categories.

3. Label each pedestal with a part-of-speech category.

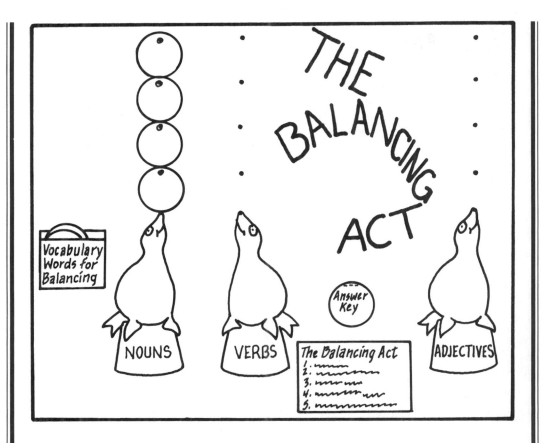

4. Make a circle pattern (use a saucer) and cut out one ball for each vocabulary word on your list and two extra balls.

5. Print the vocabulary words on the balls. Punch a hole in the top of each ball to hang it from a pushpin.

6. Print Answer Key on one of the extra balls and print the answers on the other. Place the Answer Key ball on top of the answers and staple them in position on the bulletin board. Staple only the top of the Answer Key ball, so that it can be folded up to read the answers.

7. Position and staple the pedestals and seals on the bulletin board. Place four pushpins in a vertical row over the nose of each seal.

8. Make a pocket to hold the vocabulary balls. Fold a piece of 8½-by-11-inch paper almost in half and staple along the edges, forming a pocket. Print Vocabulary Words for Balancing on the pocket. Staple the pocket in position on the bulletin board.

9. Prepare the caption and staple it in position on the bulletin board.

10. Print the following directions on a piece of 8½-by-11-inch paper:

The Balancing Act

1. Take the balancing words from the pocket.
2. Look up each word as fast as you can in the dictionary to find the part of speech.
3. When you find the part of speech, hang the ball over the correct seal.
4. Check your answers with the answer key.
5. Return the balancing words to the pocket when finished.

Games
N-V Bingo

OBJECTIVE The students will use their dictionaries to locate parts of speech of words.

DESCRIPTION This is a board game for four players. A word card is drawn, and the dictionary is used to check its part of speech.

SUGGESTIONS FOR USE This game is not difficult, so it lends itself to any part of the unit.

MATERIALS
- two pieces of 18-by-24-inch tagboard
- 64 3-by-5-inch index cards

PROCEDURE

1. Tape the two pieces of tagboard together along the 18-inch sides without overlapping the edges.

2. Duplicate the game sheet.

N-V BINGO			
N.	V.	ADJ.	ADV.

3. Make a board using four game sheets, with a rectangle in the center for the word cards.

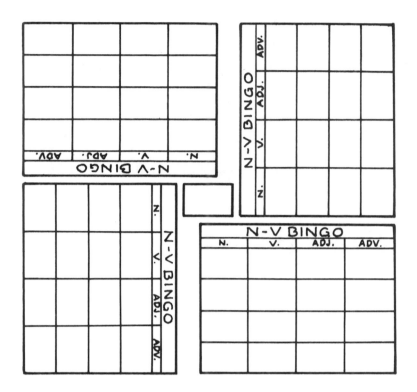

4. Label the columns N, V, Adj, and Adv as shown.

5. Cut the index cards to fit the grid spaces. You will need 64 cards. Print an unusual word on each card. (See the list of suggestions below.)

6. Provide four dictionaries at the game table.

7. Explain the following rules to the players, or print them on a piece of paper for the game table:

    a. The object of the game is to be the first to complete the grid. *(This may be changed to the first to make a complete row diagonally, horizontally, or vertically.)*

    b. The player whose first name is last in the alphabet goes first.

    c. The first player draws a word card, finds its dictionary entry, and places it under the correct heading for its part of speech on his or her board.

    d. Once a card is placed on the board, it cannot be moved.

    e. The play continues in a clockwise direction until someone has a Bingo!

    f. Cards that cannot be played are discarded.

8. *Variation #1:* Write a sentence for each word. The part of speech must be guessed before the dictionary is checked. If the player is correct, the word card is kept. If the player is incorrect, the card goes in the discard pile. A row in any direction wins.

9. *Variation #2:* Increase the difficulty factor by adding a fifth column, titled Prep, and a fifth row to each game sheet. Make 36 more word cards using words from the list of prepositions on the next page.

WORD LIST (There are approximately the same number of nouns, verbs, adjectives, and adverbs. Some words serve as more than one part of speech.)

abash (v)
abstruse (adj)
abyss (n)
afresh (adv)
babble (n or v)
babushka (n)
beastly (adj)
belligerently (adv)
chide (v)
chronicle (n or v)
collectively (adv)
compassion (n)
complacent (adj)
comprise (v)
concurrently (adv)
conglomerate (n or v)
cornice (n)
corporeal (adj)
corroborate (v)
cozily (adv)
dais (n)
darkling (adv or adj)
dauntless (adj)
echelon (n)
edgeways (adv)
educe (v)
effete (adj)
folio (n)
forensic (adj)
fumigate (v)
furthermore (adv)
galore (adv)
genial (adj)

gilded (v or adj)
grackle (n)
hapless (adj)
hark (v)
hereunto (adv)
huckster (n)
idly (adv)
idyllic (adj)
impasse (n)
impinge (v)
jabot (n)
jangle (v)
jubilant (adj)
justifiably (adv)
kindle (v)
knightly (adj or adv)
knurl (n)
larval (adj)
legibly (adv)
lexicon (n)
limn (v)
listlessly (adv)
mandarin (n or adj)
mandatory (adj)
mingle (v)
moreover (adv)
nadir (n)
notorious (adj)
nowadays (adv)
nullify (v)
opulent (adj)
outrider (n)
overboard (adv)

overwhelm (v)
palatable (adj)
prate (v)
probity (n)
profusely (adv)
qualm (n)
quarterly (n or adv)
quaver (n or v)
quotable (adj)
rendition (n)
rightful (adj)
rile (v)
ruefully (adv)
salutation (n)
sapient (adj)
satirize (v)
somehow (adv)
tenet (n)
thresh (v)
titanic (adj)
torpidly (adv)
ultraviolet (n or adj)
umber (n or adj)
unravel (v)
uptown (adj or adv)
valorous (adj)
vassal (n)
verify (v)
wither (v)
wrongly (adv)
yonder (adv)
zesty (adj)
zircon (n)

PREPOSITION LIST

about, above, across, against, along, among, around, at, before, behind, below, beneath, beside, between, beyond, by, during, for, from, in, inside, into, like, near, of, off, on, onto, over, through, throughout, till, to, toward, under, until, up, upon, with, within, without

Building Blocks

OBJECTIVE The students will use prefixes, suffixes, and root words to make derived and inflected forms.

DESCRIPTION This is a dice game for a small group of players.

SUGGESTIONS FOR USE This game is appropriate any time you wish your group to practice building words.

MATERIALS
- Diction Harry's hat or an oatmeal container, for a dice cup
- tagboard
- scissors
- white glue
- dictionary, paper, and pencil for each player

PROCEDURE
1. Cut out three 2-inch cubes out of tagboard, following the pattern.

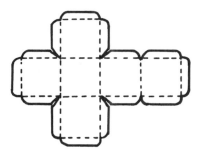

    2. Print the following root words on the faces of one cube: joy, build, value, press, print, part.

    3. Print the following prefixes on the faces of the second cube: re-, in-, dis-, mis-, de-, en-.

    4. Print the following suffixes on the faces of the third cube: -ing, -s, -ed, -ion, -ment, -ble.

    5. Score the cubes on the fold lines, fold, and glue the tabs.

    6. Supply a dictionary, a piece of paper, and a pencil for each player.

    7. Explain the following rules:
      a. The object of the game is to make the most points by building words.
      b. The person whose last name is first in the alphabet rolls the blocks first.
      c. The player writes the longest word possible using the prefix, root, and suffix showing on the top faces.
      d. The dictionary is checked to be sure the word is correct. The player earns one point for each letter.
      e. Play moves clockwise.
      f. The winner is the first player to make 150 points.

Parts of Speech and Inflected Forms Pretest

A. Write the full name of the part of speech for each abbreviation below.

1. n. _____   5. prep. _____

2. v. _____   6. conj. _____

3. adv. _____   7. pron. _____

4. adj. _____   8. interj. _____

B. Read each sentence below. Use the correct inflected form of the given word to complete each sentence.

1. What is the _____ song you know?
   (long)

2. She is even _____ than her sister.
   (beautiful)

3. Where did I _____ down my pencil?
   (lay)

4. Where will you be _____ this summer?
   (travel)

5. What is the largest fish you ever _____?
   (catch)

C. Many words are not listed as main entries in the dictionary. Put a check beside each word below that would be a main entry.

____ 1. birds   ____ 6. trashcan

____ 2. untied   ____ 7. singing

____ 3. pretest   ____ 8. whatsoever

____ 4. pretty   ____ 9. relented

____ 5. sorrier   ____ 10. griminess

What Am I?

Read the symbols below that the dictionary uses to tell you what part of speech a word is.

n	noun	*pron*	pronoun
v, vb, vt, or *vi*	verb	*prep*	preposition
adj	adjective	*conj*	conjunction
adv	adverb	*interj*	interjection

In a dictionary entry, the part of speech follows the phonetic spelling.

Example: **plate** /plāt/ *n*

A. What am I? Find the dictionary entry for each word below. Write the abbreviation and the name for the part of speech in the blanks after each pronunciation.

1. balmy /'bäm ē/ _____ _____

2. beneath /bi 'nēth/ _____ _____

3. beneath /bi 'nēth/ _____ _____

4. bravely /'brāv lē/ _____ _____

5. because /bi 'koz/ _____ _____

6. bah /'bä/ _____ _____

7. bat /bat/ _____ _____

8. bat /bat/ _____ _____

B. Use your dictionary to find an example of each part of speech below.

1. noun _____   5. adverb _____

2. verb _____   6. preposition _____

3. pronoun _____   7. conjunction _____

4. adjective _____   8. interjection _____

Regular or Irregular?

The dictionary usually does not show the principal parts of regular verbs. The *-ed* and *-ing* forms are shown only when there are spelling changes.

Example: **make** /māk/ *v* **made** /mād/; **mak·ing** /'mā king/

A. Use your dictionary to find and write the principal parts of each word below. If the principal parts are not shown, just add <u>-ed</u> and <u>-ing</u>.

1. mingle _____ _____

2. miss _____ _____

3. mislead _____ _____

4. mistake _____ _____

The dictionary shows other inflected and derived forms, often at the end of the main entry. This is called the *run-on* entry.

Example: **ea·ger** /'ē gər/ *adj:* marked by keen, enthusiastic, or sharply expectant desire or interest— **ea·ger·ly** *adv*—**ea·ger·ness** *n*

B. Use your dictionary to find two other forms of each word below. Write the forms in the blanks.

1. electric _____ _____

2. exquisite _____ _____

3. earth _____ _____

4. ecology _____ _____

The dictionary also shows the *comparative* and *superlative* forms of adjectives.

Example: **bad** *adj* **worse, worst**

C. Use your dictionary to find the comparative and superlative forms of the adjectives below. If the forms aren't listed, simply add *-er* to form the comparative and *-est* to form the superlative.

1. short *adj* _____ _____

2. scary *adj* _____ _____

3. slimy *adj* _____ _____

Noun or Verb?

A. Some words can be used as nouns *or* verbs. The pronunciation may change, too. Find the entries for each underlined word below and choose the one that matches the way the word is used in the sentence. Copy the correct phonetic spelling and write *n* or *v* to show the part of speech.

_____ ___ 1. My aunt gave me a birthday <u>present</u>.

_____ ___ 2. Who will <u>present</u> the awards?

_____ ___ 3. That <u>record</u> sold three million copies.

_____ ___ 4. <u>Record</u> your answers in the blanks.

_____ ___ 5. The soldier earned a good <u>conduct</u> medal.

_____ ___ 6. The band director will also <u>conduct</u> the chorus.

B. Find each word listed below in your dictionary. Write the abbreviation for the part of speech in the blank next to each word.

_____ 1. confetti   _____ 6. but

_____ 2. nevertheless   _____ 7. crosswise

_____ 3. lofty   _____ 8. economy

_____ 4. theirs   _____ 9. transport

_____ 5. oh   _____ 10. high-spirited

C. Look up each word below in your dictionary. Write the part of speech and the meaning for each word.

1. prestidigitation _____ _____

2. apprehensively _____ _____

3. jeopardized _____ _____

4. zirconium _____ _____

Carrots. Beets. and Other Roots

Sometimes you have to dig to find a root—a root word, that is! The dictionary uses the root word as the main entry. If you want to check the spelling or meaning of the word <u>inflected</u>, look for its root word, <u>inflect</u>.

A. Write the root word the dictionary would use as the main entry for each word below. You may use your dictionary if you are not sure.

1. radishes _____   3. blossoming _____

2. hotter _____   4. seedless _____

After you find the main entry for the root word, you will need to read the meaning for the root word. The meaning for the inflected form can be understood from the meaning for the root word.

B. Write the root word for each word below. Find the meaning for the root word and then write your own meaning for the inflected form.

1. perennially _____   _____

2. vegetating _____   _____

3. rutabagas _____   _____

4. grafted _____   _____

5. carroty _____   _____

6. organically _____   _____

C. The dictionary will usually tell you how to spell inflected forms that are *not* made by simply adding -*s, -ed, -ing, -ly*, and other suffixes. Put a check next to each word below that would be in the dictionary.

____ 1. digging   ____ 6. stoniest

____ 2. gardening   ____ 7. sunnily

____ 3. comedies   ____ 8. rooted

____ 4. tomatoes   ____ 9. muddiest

____ 5. onions   ____ 10. carried

Parts of Speech and Inflected Forms 99

Pyramids

Use the dictionary to help you build pyramids of inflected and derived forms. Use the root at the top of each pyramid and add noun and verb endings and prefixes and suffixes. Write the words in the building blocks. The first one is done for you as an example.

A.

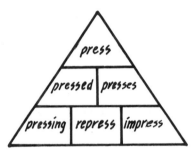

press
pressed | *presses*
pressing | *repress* | *impress*

B.

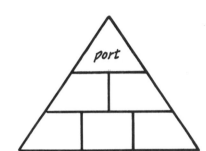

port

C.

compose

D.

form

E. Extra for Experts: Add extra rows of building blocks to pyramids A and B.

Diction Harry reproducible page, copyright © 1983

Parts of Speech and Inflected Forms Mastery Test

A. Use your dictionary to find the part of speech for each word listed below. Write the abbreviation in the blank.

_____ 1. yourself

_____ 2. gee

_____ 3. parry

_____ 4. lastly

_____ 5. thoroughbred

_____ 6. crotchety

_____ 7. because

_____ 8. among

_____ 9. foreword

_____ 10. amply

B. Use your dictionary to find the inflected forms of each word listed below. Write all the inflected forms for the words in the blanks.

1. bud, *v* _____

2. close, *adj* _____

3. noticeable, *adj* _____

4. prop, *v* _____

5. cancel, *v* _____

C. Write the root word you would find as the main entry for each word listed below.

1. defenseless _____

2. adjustable _____

3. propelled _____

4. skeptically _____

D. Put a check beside each inflected form below that the dictionary would spell for you.

1. jumps

2. lighter

3. geese

4. running

5. abilities

6. caught

Unit 9

Etymology

Objective

The students will become familiar with the etymology of our language through information given in dictionary entries.

Before You Begin

There is no pretest for this unit. It is assumed most students in grades four through seven have had little experience studying the origin of words.

Note Many classroom dictionaries do not give etymological information. Use these activities for a learning center if your supply of advanced dictionaries is limited.

Bulletin Board
Who Said It First?

OBJECTIVE The students will use the etymological information given in a dictionary to find the sources of words.

DESCRIPTION A Roman, a Frenchman, and a Native American challenge your students to find the words they have contributed to the English language.

SUGGESTIONS FOR USE Use this bulletin board to introduce etymology to your group.

MATERIALS
- overhead projector
- transparency
- pen
- sentence strips or tagboard
- scissors
- pushpins
- hole punch

PROCEDURE

1. Trace the Roman, Frenchman, and Native American onto a transparency, using the overhead projector to enlarge them to fit your bulletin board space. Trace the figures directly onto the background paper or trace them onto other paper, cut them out, and staple them in position on the bulletin board.

2. Cut out four speech balloons. Staple three of the balloons over the characters. Save the fourth balloon for the caption and directions.

3. Print words from French, Latin, and Native American languages on the sentence strips and cut them apart into individual words. Punch a hole in the top center of each card for hanging from a pushpin. Tagboard may be used instead of sentence strips. (See the list of suggested words below.)

4. Position six pushpins in each empty speech balloon.

5. Make a pocket for holding the word cards. Fold a piece of 8½-by-11-inch construction paper almost in half and staple it along the edges. Print Word Cards on the pocket and staple it in position on the bulletin board. Put the word cards in the pocket.

6. Provide a dictionary at the bulletin board.

7. Print the following directions on the fourth speech balloon:

Who Said It First?

1. Take out the word cards.
2. Use the dictionary to find out from which language we borrowed each word.
3. Hang the word cards in the correct balloons.
4. Return the word cards when finished.

WORD LISTS

1. Latin: appetite, asteroid, fiat, lunar, modern, transport
2. French: bar, cord, cuisine, fondue, omelet, racket
3. Native American: appaloosa, hammock, moose, raccoon, skunk, toboggan

Games

Roman Relay

OBJECTIVE The students will use their dictionaries to make lists of words with common roots.

DESCRIPTION Teams compete to be the first to complete a list of words with a common root. As a variation, the teams may compete to make the longest list of words with a common root. The dictionary is used as a reference.

SUGGESTIONS FOR USE This game can be used to develop vocabulary. Dictionaries with etymologies are not necessary.

MATERIALS

- Diction Harry's magic hat and wand
- sentence strips
- felt-tip pen
- scissors
- dictionary for each player
- paper and pencil for each team

PROCEDURE

1. Make three or more root word cards. Print Latin roots on sentence strips and cut the strips apart into individual words. On the back of each root word card, write the word's meaning. Place the cards in Diction Harry's hat. (See the list of suggested roots below.)

2. Divide your group into teams. The larger the team, the more difficult the game task becomes. Arrange the teams in rows.

3. Supply each player with a dictionary and the first player on each team with a piece of paper and a pencil.

4. Explain the following rules to your group:

   a. The object of the game is to be the first team to complete a list of words derived from the root word.

   b. The leader will wave the magic wand and pull a Latin root word from the hat. The meaning of the root word will be read aloud.

   c. When the leader says "Go!" the first player checks the dictionary and writes a word derived from the root. To be sure the word comes from the root, read the etymology of the word. *(If your dictionaries do not give etymologies, the player should read the meaning of the word chosen. The meaning of the English word should be related to the root word's meaning.)*

   d. The first player passes the paper and pencil back to the second player, and that player must find and write a different word. Adding *-s, -ed,* and *-ing* is not acceptable.

   e. If a player notices an error made by another player on the team, he or she may correct the error.

   f. The last player stands up to signal that his or her team's list is complete.

   g. The first team with an accurate list is the winner.

   h. Repeat the above steps with the remaining root words as time allows.

5. Variation #1: The teams may sit at tables or in groups and compete to make the longest list within a given time.

6. Variation #2: The competition may be individual. Each player competes to make the longest list in a given time.

LATIN ROOTS LISTS

1. Easy: cent, part, super, dec
2. Medium: cred, omni, pass, vale, nov, ped, reg
3. Difficult: pax, ambi, fide, curre

The Borrowers

OBJECTIVE The students will use etymologies as an aid to guessing secret words.

DESCRIPTION This game is an etymology form of Hangman.

SUGGESTIONS FOR USE Use this game at the conclusion of this unit. To be successful, the students need some knowledge of the relationships between English and its parent languages.

MATERIALS
- paper and pencil for individual play
- chalkboard or overhead projector for group play
- dictionary with etymologies for the challenger

PROCEDURE
1. Provide the players with the necessary materials.
2. Explain the following rules to your group: The game is played just like Hangman, with these additions:
   a. The language from which the word was borrowed is read from the dictionary.
   b. The meaning of the original word is given.
   For example, the challenger has chosen the mystery word *deportment*. The player would say, "From the Latin, meaning 'to carry away'."

It's All Greek to Me!

A. The English language has borrowed many words from the Greeks. *Gk* in a dictionary entry tells you the word comes from a Greek word. We owe the Greeks a lot! Read the following information about the origin of the word *television*. Circle the symbol that means *Greek*.

1. **television**
   tele- or **tel-** *comb form*   [Gk *tēle*, far off]
      1: at a distance   **2:** television

2. Use your dictionary to list words derived from tele- or tel-.

   _____

   _____

   _____

   _____

   _____

B. We also owe the Romans a lot. Their language was Latin. About 50 percent of the English language comes from Latin! Read the following information about television. Circle the symbol that means *Latin*.

1. **television**
   vision /ˈvizh ən/   *n* [L *vis-*, *vidēre*, to see]
      1: something seen as in a dream

2. Use your dictionary to list words derived from vis- and videre.

   _____

   _____

   _____

C. Name five other languages from which we have borrowed words.

   _____

...or Spanish, French, Chinese...

A. The English language has borrowed words from many languages. A dictionary uses abbreviations to tell you the origin or etymology of a word. Write the full name of the language for each abbreviation below. Use the list of abbreviations in your dictionary.

1. Gk _____   7. ME _____

2. L _____   8. ML _____

3. F _____   9. LL _____

4. OF _____   10. Sp _____

5. MF _____   11. It _____

6. OE _____   12. G _____

B. The etymology of a word follows its part of speech and may be enclosed in brackets. Circle the etymology section of the dictionary entry below.

racket   /ˈrak ət/   *n*   [MF raquette]   **1:** a light bat

C. Extra for Experts: The etymology or origin of a word may not be given in your dictionary, or there may be only a partial etymology. Match each dictionary entry below with a way of finding the etymology, or with the etymology that would actually be given for the word. Write the letter in the blank.

Entry Word

____ 1. royal blue *n*

____ 2. royalist

____ 3. rub *n* **1:** obstruction

____ 4. rubbing

____ 5. rubble

____ 6. macadam

Etymology

A. None given; see the root word.

B. Word family; see the main entry, <u>rub</u>.

C. None given; see the parts of the compound word.

D. [ME *robys*]

E. Homograph; see the other entry for <u>rub</u>.

F. [after John L. *McAdam*, d 1836, British engineer]

NAME _____

The First Americans

A. New World settlers made the Native American names for plants and animals part of their everyday language. Read the dictionary entry below.

moose /müs/ *n, pl* **moose** [of Algonquian origin]
1: a large ruminant mammal

1. Circle the part of the dictionary entry that tells where the word moose originated.
2. Find the dictionary entries for Algonquian and Algonquin. Who were the Algonquins? Where was the Algonquian dialect spoken?

_____

B. Find the dictionary entry for each word listed below and read the etymology section. If we borrowed the word from Algonquian or another Native American language, write *yes*. If we borrowed it from some other language, name the language.

_____ 1. tepee   _____ 4. corn

_____ 2. canoe   _____ 5. tomato

_____ 3. pumpkin   _____ 6. skunk

C. Use your dictionary to find the language of origin for each word in the list below. Write the name of the language next to the word.

1. buffalo _____   4. luau _____

2. patio _____   5. doctor _____

3. parka _____   6. strudel _____

D. Some words were named for the people associated with them or with their invention. Find each word below in your dictionary. Write the name of the person who gave us each word, and write the definition of the word.

1. boycott _____ _____

2. quixotic _____ _____

3. sandwich _____ _____

When in Rome

Have you heard the old saying "When in Rome, do as the Romans do"? We aren't in Rome, but we do what the Romans did every day. Many common English words come from Latin, the language spoken by the Romans.

A. Find each word listed below in the dictionary and read its etymology. For each word, write the Latin word from which it comes.

1. science _____
2. liquid _____
3. condense _____
4. precipitate _____
5. expand _____
6. evaporate _____

B. Name the language from which we most recently borrowed each of the weather words below.

1. clouds _____
2. rain _____
3. sleet _____
4. snow _____
5. hail _____
6. hurricane _____

C. A useful root word that we have borrowed from Latin is <u>port</u>. Find the entries for <u>port</u>. Use the dictionary to answer these questions.

1. From what Latin words do we get <u>port</u> as a noun and as a verb?

   a. *n* _____   b. *v* _____

2. Write at least six words that are built from the root <u>port</u>.

   _____

   _____

D. Many English words beginning with <u>con-</u> have been borrowed from Latin. Find and write at least 10 such words.

_____

_____

Diction Harry reproducible page, copyright © 1983

The Greeks Have a Word for It

When scientists name a discovery, they often borrow from Greek.

A. Read the etymology section in the dictionary for the underlined part of each word below. Write the Greek word we borrowed and its meaning.

1. <u>atom</u> _____ _____

2. <u>astronaut</u> _____ _____

3. <u>automatic</u> _____ _____

4. <u>megaton</u> _____ _____

B. Some of our borrowed words are built from two or more Greek words. Find each of the words below in the dictionary. Write the Greek words we borrowed and their meanings for each word.

1. sophomore _____ _____

_____ _____

2. biology _____ _____

_____ _____

3. helicopter _____ _____

_____ _____

4. paramecium _____ _____

_____ _____

C. Can you guess the English words we made from these borrowed words? Guess each word. Then use your dictionary to check your guesses.

Borrowed Word	Guess	Dictionary
1. ME *avengen*, fr. OF *avengier*	_____	_____
2. L *dualis*, fr. *duo* two	_____	_____
3. L *libertas*, fr. *liber* free	_____	_____

Etymology Mastery Test

A. Use your dictionary to find the origin of each word below. Write the name of the language or other source that the word comes from.

1. feminine _____

2. psychedelic _____

3. wampum _____

4. armor _____

5. habit _____

6. metropolis _____

7. autobahn _____

8. lasso _____

9. go _____

10. Celsius _____

B. Read each statement and write *true* or *false* in the blank.

_____ 1. Many words in our language come from Latin or Greek roots.

_____ 2. The first American settlers borrowed words from the Native American languages.

_____ 3. We usually change the meanings of the words we borrow.

_____ 4. Knowing the meanings of Latin and Greek roots will help you increase your vocabulary.

_____ 5. Some words come from peoples' names.

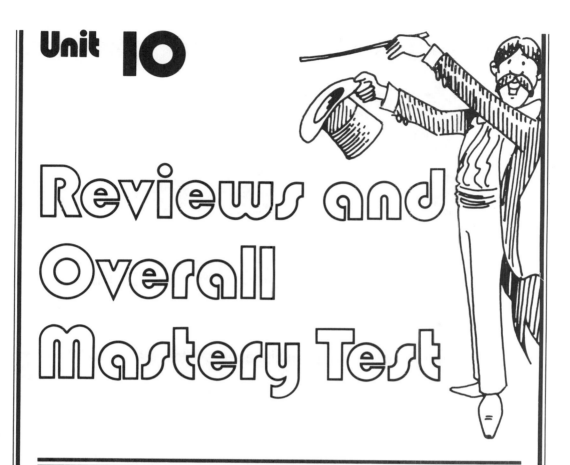

Unit 10

Reviews and Overall Mastery Test

Objective

The students will review their dictionary skills.

Suggestions for Use

Use these materials to reinforce your previous teaching and to prepare students for the overall mastery test. Each review master is keyed, in the upper left corner, to the units being reviewed.

NAME _____

Review #1

A. Number the words in each list below in alphabetical order.

1. ___ incline   2. ___ chance   3. ___ labored

    ___ steer   ___ creel   ___ labyrinth

    ___ axle   ___ cane   ___ label

    ___ lever   ___ cyst   ___ Labor Day

    ___ wheel   ___ civil   ___ laborite

    ___ gear   ___ cone   ___ laborious

B. Number the words below in alphabetical order from 1 to 10.

___ incur   ___ incurable

___ inactive   ___ icy

___ idly   ___ impact

___ inhale   ___ irrigate

___ inane   ___ itemize

C. Read each pair of guide words for a dictionary page below. Then circle the words that you would find on the page.

1. **burgeon**   **byre**

    byword   burglar   burst   bicycle   busboy

2. **director**   **disband**

    directory   dire   disappear   discover   disability

3. **post**   **posthole**

    positive   postage   postgraduate   postcard   possible

NAME _____

Review #2

A. Below is a list of questions about the solar system. Put a check next to each question for which you could find the answer in a dictionary.

____ 1. What does <u>asteroid</u> mean?

____ 2. How do you spell <u>Jupiter</u>?

____ 3. Is <u>earth</u> ever capitalized?

____ 4. Who discovered <u>Pluto</u>?

____ 5. Where can I divide <u>Neptune</u> into syllables?

____ 6. How do you pronounce <u>corona</u>?

____ 7. Where is the biggest <u>telescope</u>?

____ 8. How many moons does <u>Uranus</u> have?

____ 9. When will <u>Halley's Comet</u> reappear?

____ 10. What is the plural of <u>meteor</u>?

B. Match each part of an entry below with its name. Write the letter of the name in the blank.

Part of an Entry	Name
____ 1. **sat·el·lite**	a. synonym
____ 2. /'sat 'l īt/	b. first definition
____ 3. *n*	c. second definition
____ 4. **1:** a servile follower of a great person	d. pronunciation
____ 5. **2:** a smaller body that revolves around a planet	e. entry word
____ 6. *syn.* follower	f. part of speech

NAME _____

Review #3

A. Find the entry for <u>industry</u> in your dictionary and answer the questions below.

1. On what page do you find the entry for the word?   _____

2. What are the guide words for the page?   _____

3. Does <u>industry</u> come before or after <u>industrial</u> in the dictionary?   _____

4. What is the phonetic spelling for <u>industry</u>?   _____

5. How many syllables are there in <u>industry</u>?   _____

6. Which syllable in <u>industry</u> has the strongest accent?   _____

7. What is the plural of <u>industry</u>?   _____

8. What are two meanings for <u>industry</u>?   _____

                    _____

9. What are two synonyms for <u>industry</u>?   _____

                    _____

B. Divide these words into syllables. Then use your dictionary to mark each accented syllable.

1. about   _____

2. boomerang   _____

3. party   _____

4. parachute   _____

5. nibble   _____

NAME _____

Review #4

A. Use your dictionary to find the correct word for each phonetic spelling below. Write the words in the blanks.

1. /strāt/ _____

2. /plo͞om/ _____

3. /'dē pō/ _____

4. /ka 'fā/ _____

5. /hwak/ _____

6. /'jen trē/ _____

7. /'mäd əl/ _____

8. /'ē gəl/ _____

B. Use your dictionary to find the part of speech for each underlined word in the sentences below. Write your answers in the blanks.

1. There will be showers <u>during</u> the day. _____

2. We will <u>panel</u> the family room in oak. _____

3. The criminal had an <u>abject</u> look on his face. _____

4. The leader had a <u>kingly</u> appearance. _____

5. We were <u>practically</u> finished when the bell rang. _____

C. Use your dictionary to write two inflected forms for each word listed below.

1. tread *v* _____ _____

2. hie *v* _____ _____

3. lively *adj* _____ _____

D. Use your dictionary to find the origin of each word listed below. Write the name of the language and the original word or other source that each word comes from.

1. vertex _____

2. graham _____

3. democracy _____

NAME _____

Review #5

A. Number the words in each list below in alphabetical order.

1. ___ bell   2. ___ feather   3. ___ skillful

    ___ kite   ___ formal   ___ skate

    ___ doubt   ___ face   ___ skillet

    ___ receive   ___ finite   ___ skeleton

    ___ open   ___ flown   ___ skullcap

B. The guide words for a dictionary page are <u>division</u> and <u>doctor</u>. Circle the words below that you would find on the page.

1. dizzy   3. distance   5. dock   7. dairy   9. divine

2. do   4. doctor   6. dog   8. doorknob   10. docile

C. Neatly cross out and correct any letters that should be capitalized in the words below. Use your dictionary.

1. welsh rabbit   3. queen anne's lace   5. sarape

2. eskimo dog   4. supreme being

D. Use your dictionary to rewrite the misspelled words below.

1. adventuror   _____

2. drownded   _____

3. seige   _____

E. Use your dictionary to find a synonym for each word below.

1. consent   _____

2. curtail   _____

3. inspection   _____

Diction Harry reproducible page, copyright © 1983

Review #5 *continued*

F. Write the plural of each word below.

1. solo _____

2. deer _____

3. appendix _____

4. mother-in-law _____

G. Write a short meaning for each word below. Make sure the meaning fits the part of speech given.

1. lime *n* _____

2. lime *n* _____

3. lime *v* _____

H. Divide each word below into syllables using • and place an accent mark next to the stressed syllable.

1. faithful   2. depart   3. athletic

I. Read the joke below. Then write it on the lines, spelling the words correctly.

'tē chər: yōō shood hav ben hēr at nīn ə 'kläk.

_____

'stōōd nt: hwī, hwət 'hap ənd?

_____

J. Find the origin of each word below. Write the name of the language and the original word or other source that the word comes from.

1. cookie _____ _____

2. cardigan _____ _____

3. caribou _____ _____

Diction Harry reproducible page, copyright © 1983

NAME _____

Overall Mastery Test

A. Number the words in each list below in alphabetical order.

1. ___ diagonal   2. ___ catapult   3. ___ seclude

___ indicate   ___ cavern   ___ secretary

___ absorb   ___ cavalier   ___ second

___ facial   ___ cause   ___ secession

___ consistent   ___ cathedral   ___ section

B. The guide words for a dictionary page are <u>colon</u> and <u>come</u>. Circle the words below that would be on the page.

1. combine   4. comfort   7. colon   10. collect

2. collie   5. color   8. colony   11. comma

3. collision   6. combat   9. column   12. comedy

Use your dictionary to complete the remainder of the test.

C. Write an example for each type of entry below.

1. prefix   _____

2. suffix   _____

3. abbreviation   _____

4. single-letter entry   _____

5. compound word   _____

6. capitalized entry   _____

D. Put a check next to each question below for which you could find the answer in a dictionary.

___ 1. Who won the <u>Kentucky Derby</u> last year?

___ 2. How do you pronounce <u>ratafia</u>?

___ 3. Do you write <u>twentyfive</u> or <u>twenty-five</u>?

___ 4. What is the plural of <u>hippopotamus</u>?

___ 5. How far can a <u>kangaroo</u> jump?

120 Diction Harry

Diction Harry reproducible page, copyright © 1983

Overall Mastery Test *continued*

E. Tell whether each underlined word is used correctly or incorrectly in the sentences below. Write *right* or *wrong*.

_____ 1. The bacon <u>rime</u> was chewy.

_____ 2 The moon was <u>luminous</u>.

_____ 3. We enjoyed eating that delicious <u>croquet</u>.

_____ 4. She asked me <u>weather</u> it was raining or not.

F. Rewrite the words below, putting in capital letters where needed.

1. southern cross _____

2. fiesta _____

3. french horn _____

G. Write the plural for each word below.

1. goose _____

2. index _____

3. armful _____

H. Circle the correct American spelling of the word in each row below. There may be more than one correct spelling.

1. enroling	enroleing	enrolling
2. tranquility	tranquilety	tranquillity
3. busses	buses	buzes
4. practiceing	practising	practicing

I. Write the number of pronunciations that the dictionary gives for each word below. Then write the part of speech of each word.

1. licorice ___ _____

2. granary ___ _____

3. wherefrom ___ _____

Overall Mastery Test *continued*

J. Write two inflected forms of each word.

1. twinge   *v*   _____   _____

2. alter   *v*   _____   _____

3. droopy   *adj*   _____   _____

K. Below are some geographical names and their pronunciations. Pronounce each name. Then circle the word or phrase in each row that most nearly rhymes with the name.

1. Crete	/krēt/	cream	sleet	meter
2. Dakar	/də 'kär/	cigar	burglar	mirror
3. Milan	/mə 'lan/	island	steal in	began
4. Nantes	/nants/	can tease	pants	wants
5. Weddell	/wə 'del/	to peal	pay toll	the bell
6. Aisne	/ān/	pain	pay me	be knee
7. Baja	/'bä hä/	bay hay	bay jay	ah ha
8. Cecil	/'ses əl/	whistle	trestle	cancel
9. Quito	/'kē tō/	key two	key toe	quite oh

L. Write the name of the language of origin for each word below.

1. corrode   _____

2. crystal   _____

3. chanteuse   _____

Diction Harry reproducible page, copyright © 1983

Teacher's Notes and Answer Keys

This section of *Diction Harry* contains objectives, suggestions for use, and answer keys for the individual duplicating masters in each unit. The masters are identified by title under the appropriate unit headings.

It is assumed that the teacher has introduced key concepts and terminology, such as *parts of speech, inflections,* and *derivations,* before handing out the worksheets. The sheets themselves do not teach these concepts; they provide further illustration, practice, and reinforcement.

We strongly advise that before duplicating a worksheet, you check the answers provided in the answer key with information provided in the dictionaries your students will actually use. Answers do vary from one dictionary to another, and some dictionaries have special information or features that others do not. For example, diacritical marks and word examples in phonetic keys may vary; one dictionary may illustrate an entry word that another does not; and some dictionaries integrate entries for geographical names while others relegate that material to a special section in the back. You may need to make substitutions so that your students can arrive at correct answers using their particular dictionaries. You may also want to modify worksheets so that they assume the appropriate skills and vocabulary levels of your students.

Unit I: Alphabetizing

Pretest   page 11

OBJECTIVE   The students will demonstrate their knowledge of the alphabet and their ability to alphabetize.

SUGGESTIONS FOR USE   Have the students read the directions, and answer any questions they may have. Allow 15 to 20 minutes of working time.

ANSWER KEY
  A. The alphabet!
  B. 2. n o p   **3.** i j k   **4.** t u v
  C. 1. 3, 1, 4, 2, 5   **2.** 4, 3, 1, 5, 2   **3.** 1, 5, 2, 4, 3   **4.** 3, 2, 5, 4, 1

Sing a Song of 26-Pence! page 12

OBJECTIVE The students will reinforce and extend their knowledge of the alphabet.

SUGGESTIONS FOR USE This page may be used as a transparency to introduce alphabetizing. If you prefer to use these activities in ditto form, preview the directions with your group. Use the game Alphabet Questions, page 9, as a follow-up.

ANSWER KEY

A. **2.** QRS **3.** KLM **4.** EFG **5.** WXY **6.** OPQ **7.** TUV **8.** CDE **9.** JKL **10.** STU **11.** ABC **12.** MNO **13.** XYZ **14.** RST **15.** FGH **16.** PQR **17.** HIJ **18.** LMN **19.** GHI **20.** DEF **21.** NOP **22.** UVW **23.** IJK **24.** VWX

B. **2.** s t u **3.** c d e **4.** k l m **5.** x y z **6.** n o p **7.** i j k **8.** d e f **9.** g h i **10.** t u v **11.** h i j **12.** p q r

C. **1.** 1, 3, 5, 2, 4 **2.** 4, 1, 2, 5, 3 **3.** 5, 3, 4, 2, 1

Marching in Alphabet Time page 13

OBJECTIVE The students will review alphabetical order and use second letters to alphabetize.

SUGGESTIONS FOR USE Preview the directions. Use Diction Harry's wand as a pointer to signal important ideas.

ANSWER KEY

A. **1.** after **2.** because **3.** carry **4.** dense **5.** even **6.** feel **7.** grin **8.** hitch **9.** interest **10.** jungle **11.** knew **12.** least **13.** much **14.** never **15.** often **16.** pencil **17.** quick **18.** race **19.** since **20.** teach **21.** until **22.** very **23.** which **24.** xylophone **25.** young **26.** zoo

B. **1.** h, t, ship **2.** i, a, paper **3.** o, a, same **4.** l, o, climb **5.** i, o, divide **6.** r, i, time

C. **1.** 2, 1, 3 **2.** 2, 3, 1 **3.** 1, 3, 2

The Alphabet Two-Step and Others page 14

OBJECTIVE The students will alphabetize words using second, third, and subsequent letters.

SUGGESTIONS FOR USE Preview the directions. Use this worksheet at any time to review alphabetizing.

ANSWER KEY

A. **1.** 4, 1, 2, 5, 3 **2.** 3, 2, 5, 4, 1 **3.** 2, 3, 1, 4, 5

B. **1.** train, tree, trim, try **2.** chain, cheer, chin, chum **3.** play, plenty, plot, plum

C. **1.** 1, 2, 4, 3 **2.** 3, 1, 4, 2 **3.** 3, 4, 1, 2 **4.** 4, 1, 3, 2

The Jumbo Jumble page 15

OBJECTIVE The students will practice higher-level alphabetizing skills.

SUGGESTIONS FOR USE This page may be used as an informal check on mastery of alphabetizing skills.

ANSWER KEY

A. **1.** jack **2.** jackpot **3.** jade **4.** January **5.** jaw **6.** jelly **7.** jellyfish **8.** jester **9.** jet engine **10.** jet plane **11.** jewel **12.** jingle **13.** jostle **14.** jumper **15.** jungle **16.** junior **17.** junk **18.** justice **19.** jut **20.** jute

B. 4, 10, 9, 1, 6, 7, 8, 3, 2, 5

Mystery Messages pages 16–18

OBJECTIVE The students will use their knowledge of the alphabet to decode messages.

SUGGESTIONS FOR USE This is a three-page activity. Be sure to read the answer to the first message. Use self-stick labels and a felt-tip pen to make badges to give to students who solve the second message. Block out the last two lines of section B when you make the duplicating master if you do not have time to prepare badges.

Note: Students enjoy seeing their own work in print. Have your students write their own mystery messages and even have them make their own duplicating masters. Watch neatness and accuracy improve dramatically!

ANSWER KEY

A. The second mystery can be solved by looking under the dictionary on your teacher's desk. (*Write the following directions on a piece of paper and place them under a dictionary on your desk:* "You can decode message B by substituting the letter in the alphabet that comes *after* each letter in the message. Consider A to come after Z when you are decoding.")

B. Congratulations! You have now won the title of Master Decoder of the United States Secret Service! Your teacher has your badge.

C. *This code is a reversal code. For example, t = a and a = t. The message is:* The inventor of the telegraph, Samuel Morse, also developed the Morse code, which uses dots, dashes, and spaces. (*This mystery message is more difficult than the first two. Give less-able students a clue to unravel the code so that they do not become frustrated. Direct your students to look in an encyclopedia to find the code.*)

Alphabetizing Mastery Test page 19

OBJECTIVE The students will demonstrate their mastery of alphabetizing skills.

SUGGESTIONS FOR USE Successful completion of this test will indicate your students are well prepared for Unit 2, Guide Words.

ANSWER KEY

A. **1.** animal **2.** camel **3.** canary **4.** gnu **5.** hyena **6.** koala bear **7.** monkey **8.** parrot **9.** tiger **10.** zebra

B. **1.** canoe **2.** place **3.** birch **4.** marry **5.** cable **6.** injury **7.** hammer **8.** index **9.** table **10.** medal **11.** message **12.** perspiration

C. **1.** 6, 5, 3, 1, 2, 4 **2.** 6, 5, 4, 1, 2, 3 **3.** 5, 4, 6, 2, 3, 1

Unit 2: Guide Words

Pretest page 24

OBJECTIVE The students will demonstrate their knowledge of guide words.

SUGGESTIONS FOR USE Preview the directions with your students. Have them note that they will need their dictionaries for section C.

ANSWER KEY

A. **1, 2,** and **4** should be checked.

B. **1, 2, 3, 4, 7,** and **10** should be circled.

C. See dictionary.

Front, Middle, or Back? page 25

OBJECTIVE The students will be able to determine whether a specific word would be found in the front, middle, or back of the dictionary.

SUGGESTIONS FOR USE Use this page to develop efficiency and speed when using the dictionary. Sections A and B on the duplicating master will make the concept of *front, middle, or back* more meaningful.

Have the students turn to the exact middle of the dictionary. Have them practice turning the pages from the upper corner rather than from the lower part of the page.

Section D would make an exciting teacher-directed activity. Turn it into a contest.

ANSWER KEY
A. **1.** A, G   **2.** H, P   **3.** Q, Z.
B. **1.** back   **2.** front   **3.** middle   **4.** back   **5.** front   **6.** front   **7.** back   **8.** middle
    9. middle   **10.** back

Take Me to Your Leader! page 26

OBJECTIVE The students will locate guide words in the dictionary.

SUGGESTIONS FOR USE Use this worksheet to introduce finding guide words in a dictionary. Discuss the key concept after the students complete the worksheet. The guide words tell you quickly if the word you are looking for is on that page. They also tell you which way to go to find the word.

ANSWER KEY
A. **1—4.** See dictionary.   **5.** first   **6.** last
B. See dictionary.

Finding Words Fast page 27

OBJECTIVE The students will use guide words to locate words more quickly.

SUGGESTIONS FOR USE Tell your students to use the guide words on a page as indicators of which way to go in the dictionary. Explain that the guide words will tell you to look for your word *before* that page or *after* that page.

ANSWER KEY
A. See dictionary.
B. **1, 4, 5, 6, 8, 10, 12,** and **14** should be circled.

From Sheathe to Shield page 28

OBJECTIVE The students will use guide words to determine the location of specific words in a dictionary and will review their alphabetizing skills.

SUGGESTIONS FOR USE Use this worksheet to modify your instruction to meet individual needs. Section A should be completed by all students. Assign sections B and C to those students who have reached higher skill levels.

ANSWER KEY
A. **1.** on   **2.** on   **3.** on   **4.** after   **5.** before   **6.** on   **7.** on   **8.** on   **9.** before
    10. before   **11.** on   **12.** after   **13.** before   **14.** after   **15.** before   **16.** after
    17. after   **18.** on   **19.** before   **20.** before   **21.** on   **22.** on   **23.** before
    24. after   **25.** after   **26.** on   **27.** before   **28.** after   **29.** before   **30.** on
B. **1.** 20   **2.** 18   **3.** 12   **4.** 27   **5.** 9   **6.** 11   **7.** 19   **8.** 13   **9.** 4   **10.** 1   **11.** 17
    12. 23   **13.** 8   **14.** 30   **15.** 6   **16.** 28   **17.** 25   **18.** 22   **19.** 2   **20.** 10   **21.** 21
    22. 15   **23.** 5   **24.** 29   **25.** 24   **26.** 16   **27.** 7   **28.** 26   **29.** 3   **30.** 14
C. *gauntlet:* leather glove covered with metal plates to protect hand;   *chain mail:* armor made of metal links;   *beaver:* movable piece on helmet that protected mouth and chin;   *gorget:* piece of armor that protected throat;   *solleret:* shoe made of metal plates

Guide Words Mastery Test page 29

OBJECTIVE The students will demonstrate their mastery of the concepts and of the correct use of guide words.

SUGGESTIONS FOR USE Use the Sky Ride to Guide Words bulletin board activity to review for this test. Most students will achieve 75% or better.

ANSWER KEY

    A. **2, 3, 8, 10, 11, 12, 13, 15, 17, 18,** and **19** should be circled.

    B. **1.** alphabetical **2.** first, last **3.** guide words

Unit 3:
Getting to Know the Dictionary

Pretest page 35

OBJECTIVE The students will demonstrate their knowledge of the scope and limitations of a dictionary.

SUGGESTIONS FOR USE Administer this pretest to determine the extent of your students' knowledge and to decide which worksheets are needed to complete this knowledge.

ANSWER KEY

    A. All are yes except **7** and **10.**

    B. All are yes except **2.**

Meet Your Dictionary page 36

OBJECTIVE The students will discover some of the types of information available in their dictionaries.

SUGGESTIONS FOR USE Use this worksheet to introduce your group to their classroom dictionaries. The amount of information in a classroom dictionary will vary considerably, so even students who score high on the pretest will benefit from this activity.

ANSWER KEY

    See dictionary.

Investigate Your Dictionary page 37

OBJECTIVE The students will use their dictionaries to find specific types of information.

SUGGESTIONS FOR USE Review the skill of opening the dictionary to the exact letter you need. Review the use of guide words to find words quickly. Check your classroom dictionary to be sure the answer to question 12 is given.

ANSWER KEY

    A. **1.** possible **2.** dy•nam•ic **3.** sheaves or sheafs **4.** Answers will vary. **5.** grow (Accept other answers.) **6.** back or again **7.** gāj **8.** noun **9.** bros. **10.** zipped, zipping **11.** & **12.** Greek

SOS page 38

OBJECTIVE The students will match abbreviations and their meanings.

SUGGESTIONS FOR USE The difficulty level is minimal, and no special knowledge is needed to complete this activity.

ANSWER KEY

    A. **1.** d **2.** e **3.** a **4.** i **5.** b **6.** j **7.** g **8.** c **9.** k **10.** e **11.** b **12.** h **13.** f **14.** k

    B. Accept the old or new abbreviations.

Would You Eat a Jitney? page 39

OBJECTIVE The students will use the definition portion of dictionary entries.

SUGGESTIONS FOR USE Your students will enjoy this activity. Encourage them to invent their own questions.

ANSWER KEY

    A. 1. no **2.** no **3.** anything fancy **4.** no **5.** no **6.** yes **7.** Answers will vary.
        8. yes **9.** the student's nickname **10.** no

Getting to Know the Dictionary
Mastery Test page 40

OBJECTIVE The students will demonstrate their understanding of the scope and limitations of a dictionary.

SUGGESTIONS FOR USE Your students should have no difficulty with this worksheet.

ANSWER KEY

    A. 1. true **2.** true **3.** false **4.** true **5.** false **6.** false **7.** false **8.** true **9.** true
        10. true
    B. See dictionary.

Unit 4:
Understanding Dictionary Entries

Pretest page 47

OBJECTIVE The students will demonstrate their understanding of dictionary entries.

SUGGESTIONS FOR USE Use the pretest to determine what your students need to know about the types of dictionary entries and the parts of a dictionary entry.

ANSWER KEY

    A. All should be checked except **7.**
    B. 1. no **2.** second **3.** verb **4.** three **5.** contradict *or* disown

Dictionary Entries Match Game page 48

OBJECTIVE The students will become familiar with the types of dictionary entries.

SUGGESTIONS FOR USE Use this worksheet with those students who did not achieve satisfactorily on section A of the pretest. These students may need a review of the terms used, for example, *hyphen* and *compound*.

ANSWER KEY

    A. 1. A **2.** F **3.** I **4.** G **5.** D **6.** E **7.** B **8.** H **9.** C **10.** J
    B. Answers will vary.

Under the Microscope page 49

OBJECTIVE The students will become familiar with the parts of a dictionary entry and the function of these parts.

SUGGESTIONS FOR USE Introduce this worksheet by using the Dictionary Entry Puzzle game on pages 44–45.

ANSWER KEY

    A. 1. entry word **2.** pronunciation **3.** abbreviation for the part of speech **4.** definition
        5. abbreviation for the part of speech **6.** how the word is used
    B. Answers will vary.
    C. 1 and **3** should be circled.

Webster's Assistant page 51

OBJECTIVE The students will develop an understanding of a lexicographer's job.

SUGGESTIONS FOR USE Use the introductory paragraphs as class discussion material. Put Noah Webster into historical perspective by asking your group to name some of his American contemporaries, such as George Washington, Thomas Jefferson, and Benjamin Franklin.

ANSWER KEY

A. 1, 2, and **3.** Answers will vary. **4.** The first settlers needed new words to describe the new things they encountered in America. They borrowed some of these words from Native Americans.

B. Answers will vary.

Understanding Dictionary Entries
Mastery Test page 52

OBJECTIVE The students will demonstrate their mastery of the parts and the functions of the parts of a dictionary entry.

SUGGESTIONS FOR USE Use the game Hold Up! (pages 45–46) as preparation for this test.

ANSWER KEY

A. stop•light /'stäp lĭt/ n 1: a light on the rear of a motor vehicle that lights when the driver uses the brake pedal 2: a signal light used in controlling traffic

B. 1. true **2.** true **3.** false **4.** true **5.** false **6.** true **7.** false **8.** true **9.** true **10.** true

Unit 5:
Finding the Meanings of Words

Pretest page 58

OBJECTIVE The students will determine the meaning of a word from its context.

SUGGESTIONS FOR USE Use your students' levels of achievement to decide which activities to present and to determine how much teaching time is needed.

ANSWER KEY

A. 1. a or b **2.** f **3.** b **4.** d **5.** c **6.** a or b **7.** d or e

B. 1. plan **2.** travel **3.** group

It All Depends... page 59

OBJECTIVE The students will determine the meanings of words from their contexts.

SUGGESTIONS FOR USE Use this activity with those students who need practice. The game Guess Again! (pages 56–57) correlates with this activity.

ANSWER KEY

(Wording will vary from dictionary to dictionary.)

A. 1. a weapon used to shoot arrows **2.** bend the head or body **3.** the forward part of a ship **4.** a knot formed by doubling ribbon into one or two loops

B. 1. conceal with the hand **2.** having a slim build **3.** solid pieces of some material with one or more flat sides **4.** having a flat or even surface

Which Witch is Which? page 60

OBJECTIVE The students will use the definition portion of entries to find meanings or synonyms for words.

SUGGESTIONS FOR USE Stress section B in a class discussion.

ANSWER KEY

  A. **2.** True. A *transport* is a vehicle.   **3.** False. A *plover* is a bird.   **4.** True. *Somber* means dull or dark-colored.

  B. Answers will vary.

  C. Accept any correct meanings.

Picture Riddles page 61

OBJECTIVE The students will use their dictionaries to match pictures and words.

SUGGESTIONS FOR USE Use this activity any time. The difficulty level is minimal.

ANSWER KEY

  1. wombat, b   **2.** plaid, f   **3.** pistil, a   **4.** nosegay, d   **5.** derby, h   **6.** whippet, c   **7.** sloop, g   **8.** ketch, e

Substitutions page 62

OBJECTIVE The students will use the meaning function of dictionary entries to find substitutes for overworked words.

SUGGESTIONS FOR USE Follow up this activity with a writing assignment. Have your students check for overworked words and use their dictionaries to find substitutes.

ANSWER KEY

  A. Answers will vary.

  B. Answers will vary.

  C. **1.** guile   **2.** gudgeon   **3.** garble   **4.** garish

Finding the Meanings of Words
Mastery Test page 63

OBJECTIVE The students will use the meaning function of dictionary entries to find definitions for words.

SUGGESTIONS FOR USE Students who do not perform up to your expectations on this test may need more practice in using context to determine word meanings.

ANSWER KEY

  (These definitions may differ from the ones in your students' dictionaries.)

  A. **1.** quiet   **2.** without motion   **3.** yet

  B. Answers will vary.

  C. **1.** hunt; pursuit; ornament   **2.** sea animal; special identifying mark; certify or authenticate

Unit 6:
Syllables, Accents, and Spellings

Pretest page 69

OBJECTIVE The students will demonstrate their understanding of using the dictionary to find syllabications, accents, and spellings.

SUGGESTIONS FOR USE Missed items call for your emphasis when presenting the rest of the material in this unit.

ANSWER KEY

  A. **1.** true   **2.** true   **3.** true   **4.** true   **5.** false   **6.** false

  B. **1.** di   **2.** prob   **3.** gret   **4.** ex, ma

  C. **1.** monkeys   **2.** ranches   **3.** glasses   **4.** spies   **5.** boxes

Be SAS·sy page 70

OBJECTIVE The students will identify and use the syllable and accent marks peculiar to their dictionaries.

SUGGESTIONS FOR USE Introduce this activity by playing the game Break an Egg, page 68.

ANSWER KEY

    A, B, and **C.** See dictionary.
    D. 1. 'moun·tain **2.** vol·'can·ic **3.** ge·'ol·o·gy **4.** 'mag·ma **5.** 'at·mos·ˌphere
      6. cone
    E. dormant, eruption, devastated, monitoring

Picture It! page 71

OBJECTIVE The students will use their dictionaries to find the correct spellings of words represented by pictures.

SUGGESTIONS FOR USE For your students with auditory discrimination difficulties, supply the first three letters of each word. Use section B to review rules for forming plurals.

ANSWER KEY

    A. 1. squirrel **2.** gorilla **3.** bottles **4.** player **5.** building **6.** vegetable
      7. watermelon **8.** motorcycle *or* motorbike
    B. 1. geese **2.** mosquitoes **3.** journeys **4.** hooves **5.** mothers-in-law
      6. piccolos **7.** sheep **8.** jalopies

Flying High or Low page 72

OBJECTIVE The students will practice using their dictionaries' patterns for showing syllables and primary and secondary accents.

SUGGESTIONS FOR USE Review the use of guide words to locate entries quickly.

ANSWER KEY

    A. 1. 'en·gine **2.** 'pis·ton **3.** 'rud·der **4.** 'pi·lot **5.** 'hang·ar **6.** pro·'pel·ler
      (See dictionary for page numbers.)
    B. See dictionary.
    C. 1. ˌen·gi·'neer **2.** 'round·ˌhouse **3.** con·'duc·tor **4.** ca·'boose **5.** 'tick·et
      6. con·'trol·ler
    D. 1. 'air·ˌline **2.** 'air·ˌplane **3.** 'air·ˌstrip **4.** 'air·'tight **5.** 'air·'mail
      6. 'air·ˌport; 4 and 5 should be circled.

Write it Right! page 73

OBJECTIVE The students will use their dictionaries to locate the correct spellings of words.

SUGGESTIONS FOR USE Words that often are spelling or usage demons were chosen for this activity. Most students will benefit.

ANSWER KEY

    A. 1. separate **2.** beautiful **3.** excellent **4.** canoe **5.** athletic **6.** scissors
    B. 1. picnicked, picnicking **2.** sought, seeking **3.** swam, swum, swimming **4.** dived
      or dove, diving **5.** skied, skiing
    C. 1. worse, worst **2.** denser, densest **3.** comelier, comeliest

Syllables, Accents, and Spelling Mastery Test page 74

OBJECTIVE The students will demonstrate their mastery of the concepts and skills in this unit.

SUGGESTIONS FOR USE Reteach indicated areas of weakness. Verify the answers to section C with your classroom dictionary.

    A. 1. true **2.** false **3.** true **4.** false **5.** true **6.** false
    B. 1. ′ar•du•ous **2.** ba•′zaar **3.** ₎con•fir•′ma•tion **4.** ₎en•ter•′tain•er
    C. 1. money or monies **2.** jacks-of-all-trades **3.** trout or trouts **4.** trustees
    5. phenomena or phenomenons

Unit 7:
Using the Pronunciation Key

Pretest page 80

OBJECTIVE The students will demonstrate their knowledge of pronunciation key usage.

SUGGESTIONS FOR USE Use the results of this pretest judiciously. Pronunciation keys vary from dictionary to dictionary, and students' performances may reflect this.

Note: The diacritical marks in this portion of the answer key may not match those in your classroom dictionaries.

    A. 1. /sīt/ **2.** /kām/ **3.** /bāz/ **4.** /′sit ər/ **5.** /′jī ənt/
    B. 1. cage **2.** still **3.** neck **4.** phone **5.** cheek
    C. 1. tow, show, hoe **2.** cat, sack, chrome, sake **3.** fool, to, blue, knew **4.** gem, edge, ginger, jam **5.** sew, cinder, single

Using Key Words page 81

OBJECTIVE The students will locate and use the pronunciation keys in their dictionaries.

SUGGESTIONS FOR USE Be sure your students note that there is a shortened pronunciation key at the bottom of each pair of facing dictionary pages.

    A. See dictionary.
    B. **1, 2, 4, 6,** and **7** should be circled.
    C. See dictionary.

Fə ′net iks page 82

OBJECTIVE The students will use the pronunciation key to pronounce known and unknown words.

SUGGESTIONS FOR USE Use Caesar's Salve (page 78) to introduce this activity.

    A. 1. /laf/ **2.** u **3.** f
    B. See dictionary.
    C. 1. fight **2.** dredge **3.** mope **4.** thought **5.** wait, weight
    D. See dictionary.

Phonetic Jokes page 83

OBJECTIVE The students will use a pronunciation key to decipher riddles.

SUGGESTIONS FOR USE This fun activity is an easy review of phonetic spellings. Have the students write their own phonetic jokes to be reproduced.

    A. Boy: What's that string tied around your finger for? Girl: To remind me to mail a letter. Boy: Did you mail it? Girl: I forgot to write it!
    B. Doctor: What happened to you? Patient: I threw a horseshoe over my shoulder. Doctor: So? Patient: There was a horse nailed to it!

Phonetic Riddles page 84

OBJECTIVE The students will use their knowledge of the pronunciation key to unlock riddles.

SUGGESTIONS FOR USE Use this activity any time you feel your students are comfortable with the pronunciation key. Encourage your students to write their own riddles and even to produce their own duplicating masters.

ANSWER KEY

1. Q: What did the tide say as it left the beach? A: Nothing, it just waved. **2.** Q: Why did the teacher wear sunglasses? A: Because her class was so bright. **3.** Q: What was the turtle doing on the freeway? A: About three miles an hour. **4.** Q: When is it impossible to buy a ticket to the moon? A: When the moon is full. **5:** Q: If you find Darth Vader, Dracula, Frankenstein, and a witch doctor on your doorstep, what should you do? A: Hope it's Halloween.

Môr Fə'net iks page 85

OBJECTIVE The students will use the phonetic spellings for given words to determine regional pronunciations and will review the concept that written and spoken syllables may not match.

SUGGESTIONS FOR USE This activity calls for a high level of auditory discrimination. Section A may cause difficulty for some students.

ANSWER KEY

  A. See dictionary.
  B. 1. 2 **2.** 1
  C. 1. no **2.** yes **3.** yes **4.** yes **5.** no **6.** yes
  D. Why were the little sneakers unhappy? Their father was a loafer.

Using the Pronunciation Key
Mastery Test page 86

OBJECTIVE The students will demonstrate their mastery of the pronunciation key.

SUGGESTIONS FOR USE Students who have successfully completed Fə 'net iks (page 82) should experience no difficulty completing this exercise.

ANSWER KEY

  A. 1. true **2.** false **3.** true **4.** false **5.** true
  B. 1. k **2.** ə **3.** t **4.** z **5.** ä **6.** f **7.** kw **8.** j **9.** ā **10.** ȯ
  C. 1. /'drān ˌpīp/ **2.** /stāj/ **3.** /'ser kəl/ **4.** /'jər nē/ **5.** /läts/

Unit 8:
Parts of Speech and Inflected Forms

Pretest page 95

OBJECTIVE The students will demonstrate their knowledge of the uses of the part-of-speech and inflected-forms functions of the dictionary entry.

SUGGESTIONS FOR USE Speech patterns have a bearing on the completion of part B. Students who perform poorly on this section will benefit greatly from this unit.

ANSWER KEY

  A. 1. noun **2.** verb **3.** adverb **4.** adjective **5.** preposition **6.** conjunction
     7. pronoun **8.** interjection
  B. 1. longest **2.** more beautiful **3.** lay **4.** traveling *or* travelling **5.** caught
  C. 3, 4, 6, and **8** should be checked.

What Am I? page 96

OBJECTIVE The students will use dictionary symbols to name the parts of speech for words.

SUGGESTIONS FOR USE Make a transparency from this master and use it as a directed lesson. Have a "Who can find it first?" contest to spark interest and review finding words quickly.

ANSWER KEY

A. **1.** adj, adjective **2** and **3.** adv, adverb; prep, preposition **4.** adv, adverb **5.** conj, conjunction **6.** interj, interjection **7** and **8.** n, noun; v, verb

B. Answers will vary.

Regular or Irregular? page 97

OBJECTIVE The students will find principal parts of verbs and inflected and derived forms of dictionary entry words.

SUGGESTIONS FOR USE Make a transparency from this master and use it as a directed lesson.

ANSWER KEY

A. **1.** mingled, mingling **2.** missed, missing **3.** misled, misleading **4.** mistook, mistaken

B. Answers will vary.

C. **1.** shorter, shortest **2.** scarier, scariest **3.** slimier, slimiest

Noun or Verb? page 98

OBJECTIVE The students will use the dictionary entry to determine parts of speech for words in and out of context.

SUGGESTIONS FOR USE Careful reading is required for part A.

ANSWER KEY

A. **1.** n **2.** v **3.** n **4.** v **5.** n **6.** v (See dictionary for phonetic spellings.)

B. **1.** n **2.** adv **3.** adj **4.** pron **5.** interj **6.** conj **7.** adv **8.** n **9.** n *and* v **10.** adj

C. **1.** n, sleight of hand **2.** adv, fearfully **3.** v, exposed to danger **4.** n, a metallic element

Carrots, Beets, and Other Roots page 99

OBJECTIVE The students will use the root word of a given word to find the dictionary entry for the given word.

SUGGESTIONS FOR USE This activity revolves around an important concept. Be sure your students read and understand the introduction to part A.

ANSWER KEY

A. **1.** radish **2.** hot **3.** blossom **4.** seed

B. **1.** perennial, yearly **2.** vegetate, growing like a plant **3.** rutabaga, turnips **4.** graft, joined **5.** carrot, like a carrot in color **6.** organic, in a way that involves living organisms

C. **1, 3, 4, 6, 7, 9,** and **10** should be checked, but your classroom dictionaries may differ.

Pyramids page 100

OBJECTIVE The students will use their dictionaries to find inflected forms for root words.

SUGGESTIONS FOR USE This activity may be used as a directed teaching lesson for less-able groups.

ANSWER KEY

Answers will vary. Accept any correctly spelled words that use the given roots.

Parts of Speech and Inflected Forms
Mastery Test page 101

OBJECTIVE The students will demonstrate their understanding of the part-of-speech and inflected-form sections of dictionary entries.

SUGGESTIONS FOR USE Administer this test when your students have completed the activities in this unit.

ANSWER KEY

A. **1.** pron **2.** interj **3.** v **4.** adv **5.** n *or* adj **6.** adj **7.** conj **8.** prep **9.** n
   10. adv
B. **1.** budded, budding **2.** closer, closest **3.** noticeably **4.** propped, propping
   5. canceled *or* cancelled; canceling *or* cancelling
C. **1.** defense **2.** adjust **3.** propel **4.** skeptic *or* skeptical
D. **3, 4, 5,** and **6** should be checked.

Unit 9:
Etymology

It's All Greek to Me! page 107

OBJECTIVE The students will discover the origin of the word *television* and use their dictionaries to find other words made from the same roots.

SUGGESTIONS FOR USE This activity does not require a dictionary with etymology information.

ANSWER KEY

A. **1.** *Gk* should be circled. **2.** Some possible answers are: telecast, telecommunication, telegraph, telelens, telemeter, telepathy, telephone, telephoto, teleplay, teleprinter, telescope, telethon, teletype, teleview, and televise.
B. **1.** *L* should be circled. **2.** Some possible answers are: video, visa, visage, visible, visibility, visional, visionary, and visit.
C. Answers will vary.

...or Spanish, French, Chinese... page 108

OBJECTIVE The students will become familiar with the language abbreviations used in the etymology section of dictionary entries and with the types of etymological information given in dictionary entries.

SUGGESTIONS FOR USE This activity requires a dictionary that gives etymologies if students are to complete it independently. It also can be used as a directed lesson, for which no dictionaries are needed but which requires your guidance through the logic of deducing that *O* means "old," *M* means "middle," and so on.

ANSWER KEY

A. **1.** Greek **2.** Latin **3.** French **4.** Old French **5.** Middle French **6.** Old English
   7. Middle English **8.** Middle Latin **9.** Late Latin **10.** Spanish **11.** Italian
   12. German
B. [*MF raquette*] should be circled.
C. **1.** C **2.** A **3.** E **4.** B **5.** D **6.** F

The First Americans page 109

OBJECTIVE The students will locate the etymology of given words, with words from American Indian languages emphasized.

ANSWER KEY

   A. **1.** [*of Algonquian origin*] should be circled.   **2.** Algonquins were members of Native American tribes that spoke related languages. This dialect was spoken in the Ottawa River region of Canada.
   B. **1.** yes **2.** yes **3.** French **4.** Old English **5.** Spanish **6.** yes
   C. **1.** Italian and Spanish **2.** Spanish **3.** Aleutian, from Russian **4.** Hawaiian
   5. Latin **6.** German
   D. **1.** Charles Boycott, to engage in a joint refusal **2.** Don Quixote, idealistic, romantic
   3. John Montagu, 4th Earl of Sandwich, two or more slices of bread with a filling

When in Rome page 110

OBJECTIVE The students will find the etymologies of given words, with Latin roots emphasized.

SUGGESTIONS FOR USE A dictionary giving etymologies is needed to complete sections A and B.

ANSWER KEY

   A. **1.** scientia **2.** liquidus **3.** condensare **4.** praecipitatus **5.** expandere
   6. evaporatus
   B. **1.** Middle English **2.** Middle English **3.** Middle English **4.** Middle English
   5. Middle English **6.** Spanish
   C. **1. a.** portus **b.** portare **2.** Some possible answers are: port, portable, portal, porter, report, comport, deport, support, import, and export.
   D. Some possible answers are: concave, conceal, concede, conceive, concentrate, concentric, concept, concern, concert, conclave, conclude, concoct, concomitant, and concord.

The Greeks Have a Word for It page 111

OBJECTIVE The students will find the etymologies of words, with Greek roots emphasized. They will also use etymologies to guess English words.

SUGGESTIONS FOR USE A dictionary giving etymologies is needed.

ANSWER KEY

   A. **1.** *atomos*, "indivisible" **2.** *astron*, "star" **3.** *automatos*, "self-moving"
   4. *megas*, "large"
   B. **1.** *sophos*, "wise" and *moros*, "foolish" **2.** *bios*, "life" and *logia*, "speech, reason"
   3. *helico*, "helix" and *ptero*, "wing" **4.** *para*, "beside" and *mekos*, "length"
   C. *Dictionary:* **1.** avenge **2.** dual **3.** liberty

Etymology Mastery Test page 112

OBJECTIVE The students will demonstrate their understanding of etymological concepts and use their dictionaries to find etymologies of given words.

SUGGESTIONS FOR USE Administer this test when you feel your students are ready.

ANSWER KEY

   A. **1.** Latin **2.** Greek **3.** Algonquian **4.** Old French **5.** Latin **6.** Greek
   7. German **8.** Spanish **9.** Old English **10.** after Anders Celsius
   B. **1.** true **2.** true **3.** false **4.** true **5.** true

Unit 10:
Reviews and Overall Mastery Test

Review #1 page 114

OBJECTIVE The students will review alphabetizing skills and the function of guide words.

ANSWER KEY

A. **1.** 3, 5, 1, 4, 6, 2 **2.** 2, 5, 1, 6, 3, 4 **3.** 3, 6, 1, 2, 5, 4
B. 6, 4, 2, 8, 5, 7, 1, 3, 9, 10
C. **1.** burglar, burst, busboy **2.** directory, disappear, disability **3.** postage, postgraduate, postcard

Review #2 page 115

OBJECTIVE The students will review the use of a dictionary and the parts of dictionary entries.

ANSWER KEY

A. **1, 2, 3, 5, 6,** and **10** should be checked.
B. **1.** e **2.** d **3.** f **4.** b **5.** c **6.** a

Review #3 page 116

OBJECTIVE The students will review using the dictionary to find meanings, syllabication, accents, and correct spellings.

ANSWER KEY

A. **1, 2, 4,** and **8.** See dictionary. **3.** after **5.** three **6.** first **7.** industries
   9. Answers will vary.
B. **1.** a•'bout **2.** 'boo•mer•ang **3.** 'par•ty **4.** 'par•a•chute **5.** 'nib•ble

Review #4 page 117

OBJECTIVE The students will review using their dictionaries to interpret phonetic spellings, to find inflected forms, and to locate etymologies of words.

ANSWER KEY

A. **1.** straight or strait **2.** plume **3.** depot **4.** cafe **5.** whack **6.** gentry
   7. model **8.** eagle
B. **1.** preposition **2.** verb **3.** adjective **4.** adjective **5.** adverb
C. **1.** trod, trodden **2.** hied, hying or hieing **3.** livelier, liveliest
D. **1.** Latin, vertere **2.** after Sylvester Graham **3.** Greek, dēmokratia

Review #5 pages 118–119

OBJECTIVE The students will review the key skills involved in using a dictionary.

SUGGESTIONS FOR USE Use this review as a pretest for the final test.

ANSWER KEY

A. **1.** 1, 3, 2, 5, 4 **2.** 2, 5, 1, 3, 4 **3.** 4, 1, 3, 2, 5
B. **1, 2, 4, 5,** and **10** should be circled.
C. **1.** Welsh **2.** Eskimo **3.** Queen Anne's **4.** Supreme Being
D. **1.** adventurer **2.** drowned **3.** siege
E. Answers may vary. Possible answers are: **1.** agree **2.** shorten **3.** examination
F. **1.** solos **2.** deer **3.** appendices *or* appendixes **4.** mothers-in-law
G. Answers may vary. Possible answers are: **1.** white substance **2.** fruit or tree
   3. treat with lime
H. **1.** 'faith•ful **2.** de•'part **3.** ath•'let•ic
I. Teacher: You should have been here at nine o'clock. Student: Why, what happened?
J. **1.** Dutch, koekje **2.** after the 7th Earl of Cardigan **3.** Canadian French, from Algonquian

OBJECTIVE The students will demonstrate their mastery of key dictionary skills.

ANSWER KEY

    A. 1. 3, 5, 1, 4, 2 **2.** 1, 5, 4, 3, 2 **3.** 2, 4, 3, 1, 5

    B. 1, 5, 6, 7, 8, and **9** should be circled.

    C. Answers will vary.

    D. 2 and **4** should be checked.

    E. 1. wrong **2.** right **3.** wrong **4.** wrong

    F. 1. Southern Cross **2.** fiesta **3.** French horn

    G. 1. geese **2.** indexes *or* indices **3.** armfuls

    H. 1. enrolling **2.** tranquility or tranquillity **3.** buses or busses **4.** practicing

    I. Answers may vary. **1.** three, noun **2.** two, noun **3.** two, adverb and conjunction

    J. Answers may vary. Possible answers are: **1.** twinged, twinging **2.** altered, altering
        3. droopier, droopiest

    K. 1. sleet **2.** cigar **3.** began **4.** pants **5.** the bell **6.** pain **7.** ah ha **8.** trestle
        9. key toe

    L. 1. Latin **2.** Greek **3.** French

PART II

Library Skills

I.M.A.
BOOKSNOOP'S
Amazing
Astounding Astonishing

LIBRARY
SKILLS KIT

CONTENTS

INTRODUCTION

Welcome to *I. M. A. Booksnoop's Amazing, Astounding, Astonishing Library Skills Kit.* Everything you need to open up the world of the library and books to your students is right here between these two covers. Materials are conveniently arranged in units and include duplicatable worksheets featuring our supersleuth, I. M. A. Booksnoop, who is there to help you and your students investigate the library system and some books on the reference shelf. Here's what the kit contains:

- A statement of objectives and classroom-management suggestions for each unit.
- Blackline masters for student worksheets that develop skills needed to use the library and seven useful reference books. The worksheets are adaptable to grades 5 through 8.
- Blackline masters for a pretest and unit mastery tests.
- A blackline transparency master for each unit to help introduce new skills.
- Motivational riddles to spark interest in each unit.
- Games for each unit designed to reinforce new skills.
- Interactive bulletin board ideas that provoke initial student interest and involvement in each unit.
- A Teacher's Notes section providing a statement of objectives, suggestions for use, and an answer key for the worksheets.

Unlike other kits, *I. M. A. Booksnoop's Amazing, Astounding, Astonishing Library Skills Kit* offers flexibility and economy. Multiple worksheets are offered in each unit, so you can select what you need for your particular teaching situation. The duplicatable masters prevent you from wasting money on fancy items that can be used only once. Each page is perforated, allowing it to be easily and cleanly detached. But best of all, everything—absolutely *everything*—you need is conveniently packaged between these covers.

We strongly believe that books open new worlds for our students. That's why we want our students to experience the library as a friendly and accessible place. One way is to help them become familiar with specialized reference books—the library's tools for learning.

We also believe that increased time spent on tasks increases learning and retention, and we have designed our worksheets accordingly. Moreover, we have made each worksheet a self-contained activity that students can work on without supervision to further develop their independent work habits.

How to Use This Kit

How do you use *I. M. A. Booksnoop's Amazing, Astounding, Astonishing Library Skills Kit?* It's elementary! I. M. A. Booksnoop's prescription for motivating and improving your students' library skills is totally adaptable to your teaching needs. First, administer the pretest to determine your students' current skill levels. Then, adjusting for what your time and energy budget allow, this is what your teaching plan for a typical unit should be:

- Display I. M. A. Booksnoop's poster and the riddle to spark initial interest in the unit.
- Make and present the unit transparency to introduce a new skill.
- Duplicate the worksheets you want to use.
- Collect the necessary reference books.
- Intersperse student work periods with the correlated game.
- Construct the companion bulletin board to reinforce and extend the concepts.
- Administer the mastery test.
- Consult the Suggestions for Use section at the beginning of the unit for more ideas.

Meet the Detective. I. M. A. Booksnoop

Our detective, I. M. A. Booksnoop, will spark your students' interest in books. The Booksnoop poster and the unit riddles are designed to introduce the topics. Here's how to enlarge the I. M. A. Booksnoop poster on page 1.

MATERIALS
- posterboard or other good-quality paper
- overhead projector
- felt-tip pen
- scissors

PROCEDURE

1. Use a thermofax machine to make a transparency of the I. M. A. Booksnoop poster on page 1, or trace the design onto an overhead transparency.

2. Decide what size you want the poster to be and cut the posterboard accordingly.

3. Project the transparency and trace the poster outlines onto the posterboard with a felt-tip pen. Color the poster or invite your students to color it if you wish.

Display the finished poster with an appropriate riddle at the beginning of each unit. Here are directions for using the poster and riddles in conjunction with each unit.

MATERIALS

- enlarged I. M. A. Booksnoop poster
- piece of paper to fit inside magnifying glass on poster
- unit riddle
- pen
- pushpin

PROCEDURE

1. Print the riddle on the piece of paper.

2. Attach the riddle to the magnifying glass in the Booksnoop poster.

3. Explain to your group how you wish them to present their answers (orally or in written form).

4. Change the riddle at the beginning of each new unit.

Booksnoop Pretest

A. Alphabetical Order: Number the words in each list below in alphabetical order.

1. ___ winter   2. ___ dairy

   ___ trust   ___ deed

   ___ fragile   ___ down

   ___ canary   ___ draft

   ___ staple   ___ diner

B. Guide Words: The guide words for a page in a reference book are *pirate* and *Pluto.* Circle the words below that would be found on the page.

1. private	3. pleat	5. pistol	7. plastic
2. plate	4. piracy	6. plot	8. purple

C. Choosing Key Words: Circle the key word or words in each question below that you would look up in an index or an encyclopedia to find the answer to the question.

1. Who invented the camera?
2. What foods were eaten by the early Pueblo Indians?
3. Did Alexander the Great conquer the Egyptians?
4. Who was the first doctor to use antibiotics?
5. What products are manufactured in Alabama?

NAME _____

Booksnoop Pretest *continued*

D. Using the Library: Write *true* or *false* next to each sentence below.

_____ 1. All books in a library are arranged in alphabetical order.

_____ 2. The card catalog has three cards for each book in the library.

_____ 3. Encyclopedias and almanacs are found in the reference section of the library.

_____ 4. The Dewey Decimal System uses numbers and alphabetical order to classify books.

_____ 5. Fiction books are listed in the 800s in the Dewey Decimal System.

E. Choosing Reference Books

a. almanac
b. atlas
c. biographical dictionary
d. book of quotations
e. encyclopedia
f. geographical dictionary
g. thesaurus

Write the letter of the reference book above that would be the *best* help in answering each question below.

____ 1. What are the parts of a flower?

____ 2. Who won the Kentucky Derby last year?

____ 3. Who said, "One if by land . . ."?

____ 4. What is the area of Alaska?

____ 5. What is the capital city of Ethiopia?

____ 6. When did Thomas Jefferson live?

____ 7. Which countries border France?

____ 8. What books did Mark Twain write?

____ 9. What is another word for *cloudy?*

____ 10. What languages are spoken in India?

I. M. A. Booksnoop reproducible page, copyright © 1983

Booksnoop Pretest 7

Book/noop Prete/t *continued*

F. Using Reference Books: Write *true* or *false* next to each sentence below.

_____ 1. The table of contents is the fastest way to find a topic in a book.

_____ 2. A bibliography can tell you where to find more information.

_____ 3. To find out more about Charles Lindbergh, use Volume C of an encyclopedia.

_____ 4. An atlas has an alphabetical index of place names.

_____ 5. The biographical dictionary gives facts about famous people.

_____ 6. An almanac is published yearly.

_____ 7. The geographical dictionary will give you all the facts you need for a report about Japan.

_____ 8. A thesaurus lists synonyms (and sometimes antonyms) for many words.

_____ 9. Some encyclopedias have indexes.

_____ 10. A book of quotations lists all the sayings of an important person.

Unit 1

Alphabet Sleuth

Objective

The students will review and strengthen their alphabetizing skills and their abilities to use guide words.

Before You Begin

Use the alphabetical order and guide word sections of the pretest to determine which students will benefit from the activities in this unit. Knowledge of the alphabet and efficient use of guide words are prerequisites to success with the materials in *Booksnoop*.

Motivational Riddles
The Organizers

SUGGESTIONS FOR USE Use these riddles to introduce the alphabet and guide words as valuable tools for the quick and efficient use of reference books. Attach a riddle to the magnifying glass in the Booksnoop poster (see page 1).

RIDDLE #1
I am the organizer. I am the key!
When you use a reference book, you need me.
I'm easy to spot: *Z* is my bottom and *A* is my top.
I am the _____, you see.
   Answer: Alphabet

RIDDLE #2
When you use a reference book, it's me you should heed.
I'm on every page, and my job is to lead.
I'm always the first, and I'm always the last.
If you use me, you will find things fast!
   Answer: Guide words

Bulletin Board
Clarence Croaker and the Croakettes

OBJECTIVE The pupils will practice alphabetizing.

DESCRIPTION Various song titles and names of members of a singing group are placed in alphabetical order.

SUGGESTIONS FOR USE Use this bulletin board to review and reinforce the topics covered in Unit 1.

MATERIALS
- tagboard, 21 inches by 26 inches, seven or eight sheets in various colors
- scissors
- felt-tip pen
- pushpins
- hole punch

Clarence Croaker and the Croakettes

MELANIE GRACIE
KATY MELVINA

Alphabetize these hits.	Unscramble these hit record titles by putting the words in alphabetical order.	In what order would these be listed in the Who's Who of Music?
• Waterlogged • Croaking • Lilies • Bugaboo • Leapfrog	Crisp Baby Flies Lily Boggy Pond Leap Lake Ladybug Blue Believing Bullfrog Croaker Coy Cold	• Katy Kazoo • Melvina Moo • Melanie Mellow • Gracie Gargle • Clarence Croaker

Lift for Answers

PROCEDURE

1. Cut a lily pad and lilies out of the tagboard. Print the title on the lily pad. Staple the lily pad and lilies to the board.

2. Draw a pattern and cut out four female frogs. Staple them to the board.

3. Reverse the pattern that was used for the female frogs (omit the bow) and use it for Clarence. Trace and cut out Clarence and staple him to the board.

4. Cut four rectangles out of tagboard for the Croakettes' names. Print the names and staple them to the board.

5. Cut three more rectangles out of tagboard. Print the directions on them and staple them to the board.

6. Cut three more rectangles out of tagboard. Print the items to be alphabetized on them and staple them to the board.

7. Position pushpins next to each of the hits to be alphabetized and each name in the *Who's Who in Music* list.

8. Cut 10 circles and number the circles from 1 to 5 twice. Suspend each set of circles from a pushpin positioned under the hits and *Who's Who* lists. The pushpins hold the circles when they are not being used.

9. Print the answers on a piece of tagboard and staple it so that they will be exposed when the bottom edge of the paper is lifted.

Game
Alphabet Sentences

OBJECTIVE The students will use their knowledge of alphabetical order to organize sentences.

DESCRIPTION Teams compete to be the first to unscramble words and put them in alphabetical order to make a sentence.

MATERIALS
- scrambled sentences on tagboard sentence strips (see the sample sentences below)
- paper and pencil for each student

PROCEDURE

1. Prepare the sentence strips. Print the answers on the reverse sides for easy reference.

2. Divide your group into teams.

3. Be sure all team members have paper and pencil.

4. Explain the rules:

  a. The object of the game is to be the first team to unscramble the words by putting them in alphabetical order to make a sentence.

  b. When the sentence is written in alphabetical order on the players' papers, the players raise their hands. The teacher will ask the first player who raised a hand to read the unscrambled sentence.

  c. One point is scored for each correctly unscrambled sentence.

  d. If the player incorrectly unscrambled the words, the teacher will ask the next player who raised a hand, and so on.

  e. When all the sentences are unscrambled, the team with the highest score wins.

SAMPLE SCRAMBLES

Scrambled great Charles honor elephants drew for.
Unscrambled Charles drew elephants for great honor.

Scrambled skippers salvage sailors spy scrap sixteen scarce since secretly stealthily.
Unscrambled Sailors salvage scarce scrap secretly since sixteen skippers spy stealthily.

How to Be a Detective

A. Alphabetizing: Circle the word in each pair below that would come first in a reference book. Underline the letter that tells you.

1. Alabama *or* Alamo?
2. motorcycle *or* motorcade?
3. rhinoceros *or* rhinestone?
4. coaster *or* coast guard?
5. microbiology *or* microbe?

B. Names: Circle the name in each pair below that would come first in a reference book.

1. Alice Baker *or* Andrew Bailey?
2. Smith, John *or* Samuel, Aaron?
3. Mount Everest *or* Montevideo?
4. Amazon River *or* Mississippi River?
5. George Washington Carver *or* George Washington?

C. Guide Words: Tell whether each word below comes *before, on,* or *after* the page on which these guide words appear.

salamander   sassafras

_____ 1. sable	_____ 6. stalactite
_____ 2. stable	_____ 7. Saturn
_____ 3. Sahara	_____ 8. Salome
_____ 4. sandpiper	_____ 9. San Juan
_____ 5. saucer	_____ 10. Saskatchewan

Alphabet Clues

A. The most useful piece of equipment in your detective kit is the alphabet. Show how well you know the alphabet. Write the next three letters of the alphabet that follow each letter listed below.

1. b __ __ __   5. s __ __ __   9. e __ __ __

2. m __ __ __   6. w __ __ __   10. u __ __ __

3. d __ __ __   7. c __ __ __   11. h __ __ __

4. l __ __ __   8. i __ __ __   12. p __ __ __

B. Once you know the alphabet, it is easy to put words in alphabetical order. Number the words in each list below in alphabetical order. In the second list, look at the second letter of each word to determine the alphabetical order. In the third list, look at the third letter in each word.

1. __ menace   2. __ coffee   3. __ frail

   __ apple   __ cite   __ freeze

   __ simple   __ camper   __ friend

   __ detour   __ cube   __ frond

   __ value   __ cellar   __ fruit

C. Sometimes you will have to look at the fourth, the fifth, or even the sixth letters to decide which word comes first. Underline the word in each pair below that comes first in alphabetical order. Circle the letters in the words that help you decide.

1. straight *or* strange   6. cyclone *or* cycle

2. Pluto *or* plutonium   7. whale *or* wheat

3. Egypt *or* egoism   8. rodent *or* rodeo

4. mosaic *or* mosque   9. video *or* victory

5. Alabama *or* Alamo   10. brazen *or* Brazil

∩ame Sleuth

A. A detective must be able to locate names quickly, too! Names are placed in alphabetical order using the last names. Number the namesbelow in alphabetical order.

___ Cornwall, James   ___ Hogan, James

___ Johnson, Gerald   ___ Taylor, Samuel

___ Solomon, Susan   ___ Preston, Harry

___ Adams, June   ___ Gordon, Arthur

___ Jackson, Edith   ___ Richards, John

B. Don't be fooled when the name is written the way we normally say it—for example, *Thomas Adams.* You still use the last name to determine the alphabetical order. Number the names below in alphabetical order.

___ Ann Harrison   ___ Andrew Beckwith

___ Joel Newman   ___ Ronald Levin

___ Albert Smith   ___ George Romaldi

___ Scott Perry   ___ Charles Moore

___ Patricia Newhouse   ___ Barbara Caldwell

C. If the last names are the same, then the first names are used to determine alphabetical order. Number the names below in alphabetical order.

___ John Smythe   ___ Wilson Calhoun

___ Jerry Smythe   ___ Sally Talbot

___ Sara Talbot   ___ Julia Wilson

___ Jack Berens   ___ Jane Berens

___ Lyle Calhoun   ___ Lisa Lyons

NAME _____

The Detective's Assistant

Guide words are the detective's assistant. Most reference books use guide words to help you find entries more quickly. There are two guide words at the top of each page. By looking at the guide words, you can decide whether the word you are looking for would be on that page. Here is a sample of two guide words for a page and some of the words that would be found on the page.

camp   **candle**
campaign   Canada
camphor   Canada goose
camporee   canal

Camp is the first word on the page and *candle* is the last word listed on the page. The words listed on the page all come alphabetically between *camp* and *candle*.

A. The guide words for a page are *marble* and *Marie Antoinette*. Circle the words in the list below that would be found on the page.

Marianas Islands	market	Manchuria
music	mammoth	March
Maria Theresa	mare	Mecca
McKinley	monsters	manganese
neutron	Marburg	margarine

B. Use your own words to tell what guide words are.

_____

_____

16 **I. M. A. Booksnoop**

I. M. A. Booksnoop reproducible page, copyright © 1983

Investigating Guide Words

Guide words will tell you where to go to find the entry you want. If your word comes alphabetically before the first guide word, then you know you need to look closer to the front of the book. If the entry you want comes after the second guide word, then you know you need to turn toward the back of the book.

A. The guide words for a page are *Paris* and *Pompeii.* Tell whether each word in the list below comes before, on, or after the page. Write *before, on,* or *after* next to each word.

_____ 1. Plato   _____ 6. Poland

_____ 2. Panama   _____ 7. Peking

_____ 3. Prussia   _____ 8. Pueblo

_____ 4. Pikes Peak   _____ 9. Pacific

_____ 5. Persia   _____ 10. Pontiac

B. The guide words for a page are *Cascade* and *Cleopatra.* Circle the names in the list below that would be found on the page.

1. Clay, Henry   6. Cabot, John
2. Cape Town   7. Charles I
3. Cicero   8. Cato
4. Carroll, Charles   9. Clark, George R.
5. Churchill, Winston   10. Cleveland, Grover

C. Renumber the names in part B in alphabetical order.

Guide Word Graduate

A. The guide words for a page are *Salem* and *Scotland.* Circle the words in the list below that would be found on the page.

1. Santiago
2. Sahara
3. Siberia
4. Santa Fe
5. Saigon
6. Sidney
7. Scilly Isles
8. Scranton
9. Sonora
10. Scipio
11. Schubert, Franz
12. Saxony

B. The guide words for a page are *chevron* and *Chile.* Tell whether each word in the list below comes before, on, or after the page. Write *before, on,* or *after* next to each word.

_____ 1. Chicago
_____ 2. cheese
_____ 3. chrome
_____ 4. child
_____ 5. chetah
_____ 6. chimney
_____ 7. chieftain
_____ 8. chicle
_____ 9. Cheyenne
_____ 10. chlorine
_____ 11. Chickasaw
_____ 12. chic
_____ 13. chemical
_____ 14. chipmunk
_____ 15. checkers
_____ 16. Chief of Staff

C. Rewrite the words in part B in alphabetical order below.

_____ _____ _____ _____

_____ _____ _____ _____

_____ _____ _____ _____

_____ _____ _____ _____

NAME _____

Alphabet Sleuth Test

A. Number the words or names in each list below in alphabetical order.

1. ___ shelf

   ___ shed

   ___ sew

   ___ shatter

   ___ sheep

   ___ shave

   ___ shimmer

   ___ shock

2. ___ John Bates

   ___ Thomas Becket

   ___ Sarah Bates

   ___ Andrew Brown

   ___ Carl Bering

   ___ Benjamin Bell

   ___ Betsy Brown

   ___ Susan Byron

B. The guide words for a page are *Washington* and *Windsor.* Circle the names in the list below that would be found on the page.

1. Winchester
2. Weddell
3. Wales
4. Wisconsin
5. Warsaw
6. Virginia
7. Westchester
8. Whitehorse
9. West Indies
10. Wyoming
11. Waterford
12. White Nile
13. Washington
14. Winnipeg

Parts of a Book

Objective

The students will become familiar with the functions of the title page, the table of contents, the index, and the bibliography section and will be able to locate information in these sections of a book.

Before You Begin

Use part F of the pretest to determine whether students need to strengthen their knowledge of the parts of a book, then choose the appropriate activities. Introduce these activities by having the students leaf through fiction and nonfiction books and locate and name the parts of a book that are not part of the text. See page 118 in the Teacher's Notes section for a complete explanation of the parts of a book.

Motivational Riddles
Four Parts

SUGGESTIONS FOR USE Use these riddles to introduce this unit and to motivate the appropriate lessons. Attach a riddle to the magnifying glass in the Booksnoop poster. Use the first riddle as a group motivator and the other riddles as contests.

RIDDLE #1

You might look at me for the book name
Or the book title; it's all the same.
The illustrator you might discover
By using these clues plus another:
At the beginning I usually sit.
Guess what I am to score a hit!
  Answer: Title page

RIDDLE #2

Near or at the end you will find me,
I'm more than one page, usually!
The topics in a book I tell,
I will help you if you use me well.
Look with some care, and you'll find me soon!
  Answer: Index

RIDDLE #3

I am the names of some books in a book.
You can find me — take a look!
The alphabet helps to keep me in line.
As a source of more facts, I'm a real gold mine.
Near the end you will most often find me.
Just unlock the clues by using this key!
  Answer: Bibliography

RIDDLE #4

After the title but before the index,
After the table of contents but before the appendix,
I give credit where credit is due . . .
Another name for a simple thank you.
  Answer: Acknowledgements

Bulletin Board
All about Books

Can you find the title page?

ALL ABOUT
BOOKS
BY
I.M.A. BOOKSNOOP

OBJECTIVE The students will locate the parts of a book.

DESCRIPTION A larger-than-life book is manipulated to illustrate the various parts of a book.

SUGGESTIONS FOR USE Use this bulletin board to introduce the topics you wish to cover in Unit 2. If you plan to discuss parts of a book not covered by the duplicating masters, use this bulletin board to present them.

MATERIALS
- tagboard, 21 inches by 26 inches, three or more sheets
- transparent tape
- hole punch
- pushpins
- construction paper
- pen
- stapler

PROCEDURE

1. Tape two sheets of tagboard together along the 26-inch edge. Tape additional sheets for each part of a book you wish to present to your group.

2. Punch two holes in the top edge of each sheet, about 2 inches down from the top and 2 inches in from the outside edges. Make the holes large enough to fit easily over the head of a pushpin.

3. Use a classroom book as your model. Print a sample page for each part of a book you wish to present — title page, table of contents, index, and so on.

4. Print a challenge on a piece of construction paper: ''Can you find the _____?'' Staple it in position on the bulletin board.

5. Position two pushpins on the bulletin board, matching the distance between the holes in the book.

6. Position two more pushpins to hold the book when the pages are open. The holes in the book should rest on the heads of the pushpins. This will allow the pages of the book to be turned easily.

Game
Book Look

OBJECTIVE The students will match the information found in various parts of a book with the names of the parts.

DESCRIPTION This is a teacher-directed game. You may organize competition for team or individual play.

SUGGESTIONS FOR USE Use this game as a review.

MATERIALS
- sheet of notebook paper and pencil for each player or each team
- teacher-prepared information statements

PROCEDURE

1. Prepare information statements by listing information that would be found in various parts of a book.

2. Divide your group into teams, if desired, and provide paper and pencil.

3. Explain the rules to your group:
   a. The object of the game is to complete your game sheet.
   b. Prepare your game sheet by listing any five parts of a book. Skip a line after each part.
   c. An information statement will be read. Write the information under the correct heading. If the statement is ''Written by Irene Hunt,'' write it under Title Page, because this is where you would find it.
   d. The first person or team to complete a sheet is the winner.
   e. Make a new game sheet and we will try again.

There Are Two Sides to Every Story: The Title Page

Read this title page and its other side. Then use the information to answer the questions below.

Title Page	Other Side
Land of Many Cultures by Eric Dalton Illustrated by Margaret Batesford Fairfield Publishers New York	Copyright © 1975 by Fairfield Publishers All rights reserved. Printed in the United States of America. ISBN 0– 603– 02437– 1

1. Who wrote the book? _____

2. What is the title? _____

3. Who published the book? _____

4. Where was it published? _____

5. Who illustrated the book? _____

6. What is the date of copyright? _____

7. Is the information in the book current enough to be used for a

report? _____ Why or why not? _____

8. What is the International Standard Book Number (ISBN)? _____

_____

Sifting for Big Clues: The Table of Contents

A. Answer the questions about a table of contents below.

1. Where will you find it in any book? _____

2. Which does it tell you — the main ideas found in the book or the

   details? _____

B. Read the table of contents below. Then answer the questions.

Indians of Central America

1. What is the title of Chapter 5? _____

2. How many chapters are listed? _____

3. Which chapter would tell you about the changes the Spanish

   brought? _____

4. Which chapter would tell you about the foods grown by Indians in

   Central America? _____

5. Where would you look to find out how to pronounce

   Tenochtitlan? _____

6. Where would you look if you wanted to know if the book had

   information about the Mixtecs? _____

NAME _____

Sifting for Clues: Using the Index

Use the section of the index below to answer the questions on these two worksheets.

gauchos, 79, 82*
government, 129–135
   Argentina, in, 189
   Bolivia, in, 64
   Chile, in, 70
   collective farms, 80
   economic system
     and, 130
   Paraguay, in, 72
   political parties, 131
Guatemala, 92–93

*illustration

Guyana, 90
Havana, 25
Incas, 50–55
   capital, Cuzco, 50
   farming methods,
     52*
   government, 50
   location, 50
   mining, 54
   Spanish conquest,
     55
Indians, 35–60

astronomy, 40
Aztecs, 40–45
Brazil, in, 46
cities, 40, 50
food, 36, 42
homes, 36, 42
Incas, 50–55
languages, 41, 47
Mayas, 55–60
religion, 42, 47, 58
temples, 42,* 47,
   49,* 58, 60*

A. Use the index to answer the questions below.
On what page or pages would you find:

_____ 1. information about Brazilian Indians?

_____ 2. a picture of a gaucho?

_____ 3. the names of Indian languages?

_____ 4. the way the Incas farmed?

_____ 5. pictures of Indian temples?

_____ 6. the form of government in Bolivia?

_____ 7. what the Indians knew about astronomy?

B. Pretend you are an index maker. Number the entries below in the order in which they would appear in an index.

___ Lake Titicaca, 4

___ Mayas, 55–60

___ Isthmus of Panama, 15

___ Jamaica, 10

___ Lake Maracaibo, 4

___ industry, 20

___ Magellan, F., 65

___ currency, 38–39

26 I. M. A. Booksnoop

I. M. A. Booksnoop reproducible page, copyright © 1983

Sifting for Clues: Using the Index *continued*

C. Use the index to answer the questions below. You may need to look under more than one heading.
  On what page or pages might you find:

_____ 1. what foods the Incas ate?

_____ 2. the religions of the Indians?

_____ 3. the results of the Spanish conquest?

_____ 4. the important buildings?

_____ 5. a picture of an Inca Indian?

_____ 6. who has the right to vote in Argentina?

_____ 7. what crops are grown in Guatemala?

D. Answer the questions about indexes below.

1. How are the items in an index arranged?

  _____

2. How does an index save time?

  _____

3. How may an index tell you there is a picture of the item you are

  interested in? _____

4. What does a dash between two page numbers mean?

  _____

5. Why is an index better than a table of contents for finding items in

  a book? _____

The Informer: The Bibliography

A. Use this sample bibliography to answer the questions below.

Allred, Calvin, *Life of the Aztecs.* Boston: Purlman Publishers, 1978.
Caulfred, Henry, *Latin American Governments.* London: Atman, 1976.
Emery, Stephen, *Incas of the Andes.* New York: Smithfield Publishers, 1980.
Frankfort, Jonathan, *Spanish Conquerors.* New York: Lockman and Sons, 1976.
Hayman, Frederick, *Art and Architecture of the Mayas.* New York: Robertson
   Press, 1979.
Lernan, Alan, *The Story of Latin American Independence.* Boston: Edwards
   and Sons, 1970.

1. Would a bibliography be in the front, the middle, or the back of

   a book? _____

2. How can a bibliography help you? _____

   _____

   _____

3. In what order are books listed in a bibliography? _____

   _____

B. Use the bibliography above. Write the last name of the author of
the book or books that would:

1. have a picture of a Mayan temple. _____

2. tell you which country or countries have presidents. _____

3. probably have out-of-date information. _____

4. tell you about the Indians of Latin America. _____

   _____ _____

5. tell you how the Spanish treated the Indians. _____

6. be the most up-to-date. _____

7. tell you about the ways the Indian chiefs governed.

   _____ _____

Parts of a Book Test

A. Match each part of a book listed below with the type of information it may give you. Write the letters in the blanks. You may use a letter more than once.

Information

Part

____ 1. Author's name

a. Title page
b. Table of contents

____ 2. List of chapters

c. Copyright page
d. Index

____ 3. Copyright date

e. Bibliography

____ 4. Location of an illustration

____ 5. Books the author used as sources for facts

____ 6. The International Standard Book Number

____ 7. Books for finding more information

____ 8. Publisher's name

____ 9. Exact location of an item

____ 10. Illustrator's name

B. Read each statement below. Write *true* or *false* next to each one.

_____ 1. The title page tells you the main topics in a book.

_____ 2. The table of contents lists the chapters in the order you would find them in the book.

_____ 3. You can use the index to locate items quickly.

_____ 4. The bibliography lists the copyright dates of the books the author used.

_____ 5. The index is in alphabetical order.

C. Use this section of index to answer the questions below. There may be more than one answer to a question.

Inca empire, 28– 56
  achievements,
    55– 56
  cities in, 34
  communication, 29,
    32– 35
  date of, 28
  extent of, 28
  farming, 30– 33
  government, 37– 42
  language of, 28

population, 28
Spanish conquest,
    43– 45
transportation, 32
travel in, 29, 32– 35
unexplained
    mysteries, 55
India, 189– 235
  achievements,
    230– 235
  caste system,

210– 213
farming, 192– 195
industry, 196– 203
land use, 203
population,
    189– 191
religions, major,
    204– 212
social structure,
    210– 213

1. Which pages will tell you whether the Incas had a king or a

   chieftain? _____

2. Which pages would you look at to find out whether the Incas built

   roads? _____

3. Which pages would help you find out what the local foods of

   India are? _____

4. Under what other topic heading could you look to find out about
   the caste system? (Which topic appears on the same four pages as

   the caste system?) _____

5. On which pages would you look for a map showing the crops

   grown in India? _____

6. Where would you look to find information about the buildings the

   Incas left? _____

7. Where would you look to find the important manufacturing centers

   in India? _____

8. Where would you look to find out about irrigation channels built

   by the Incas? _____

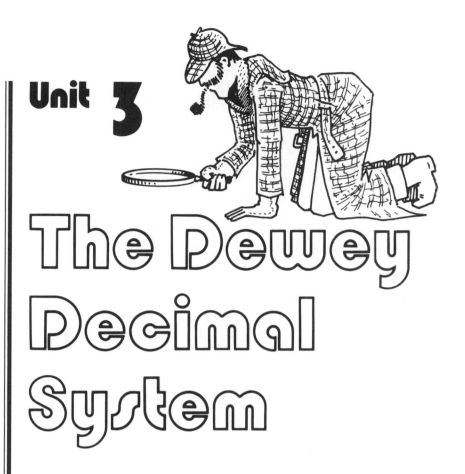

Unit 3

The Dewey Decimal System

Objective

The students will become familiar with the Dewey Decimal System.

Before You Begin

Your library may use the Library of Congress system rather than the Dewey Decimal System for cataloging and shelving books. If so, you will need to revise the numbers on Unit 3's worksheets accordingly.

Motivational Riddle
Where, Oh Where, Has My Little Book Gone?

SUGGESTION FOR USE Use this riddle as a follow-up to your teaching. Attach the riddle to the magnifying glass in the Booksnoop poster. Change the third line of the riddle as appropriate to review other portions of the Dewey Decimal System.

RIDDLE
Where, oh where, has my little book gone?
Where, oh where can it be?
I need it to learn how to play a game.
Oh where, oh where can it be?
   Answer: 700s, Arts, games, music, dancing, and painting

Bulletin Board
I. M. A. Booksnoop's Fallen Shelves

OBJECTIVE The students will use the Dewey Decimal System to classify a given set of book titles.

DESCRIPTION The students' task is to sort book cards according to their Dewey Decimal System categories. Change the book cards to update this board quickly. Increase the level of difficulty as your students' skills develop.

MATERIALS
- six sheets of tagboard of assorted colors
- I. M. A. Booksnoop poster art, page 1
- scissors
- pen
- stapler
- construction paper

PROCEDURE
  1. Reproduce I. M. A. Booksnoop by following the steps on page 5. Staple him to the bulletin board.
  2. Cut out a dialogue balloon large enough to accommodate the following message: ''I'm in trouble! All of my books have fallen from my

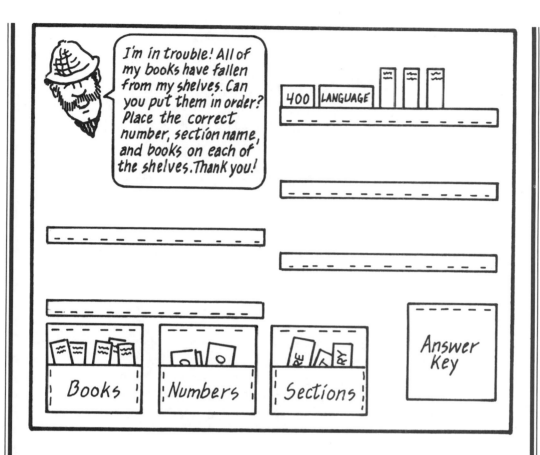

shelves. Can you put them in order? Place the correct number, section name, and books on each of the shelves. Thank you!" Staple the balloon to the bulletin board.

3. Make the shelves. Cut strips of tagboard 1½ inches wide. Staple them to the bulletin board along their lower edges. Make as many shelves as will fit on your bulletin board; space the shelves about 1 inch farther apart than the height of your books.

4. Cut ten 3-by-4-inch cards. Print a Dewey Decimal System number at the top of each card so that the number shows when the card is placed in the shelf. (See page 37 for the Dewey Decimal System classification chart.)

5. Cut ten 3-by-6-inch cards. Print a Dewey Decimal System classification name at the top of each card so that the name shows when the card is placed in the shelf strip.

6. Cut a 2-by-7-inch strip for each book title you wish to use. Print a title on each strip. Use five to seven books for each category.

7. Use three pieces of 8½-by-11-inch construction paper to make three storage pockets. Fold up the bottom third of each sheet and staple along the edges, forming a pocket. Label one pocket Numbers, one pocket Sections, and one pocket Books. Staple the pockets to the bulletin board.

8. Print an answer key on a piece of construction paper. On a matching piece of construction paper, print Answer Key. Cover the answers with this piece of paper and staple along the top only. This makes a flap that can be lifted by the students to check their work.

Game
Dewey Decimal Relay

OBJECTIVE The students will use the Dewey Decimal System to classify books.

DESCRIPTION Teams compete to be the first to correctly classify a list of book titles.

MATERIALS
- game sheet listing the Dewey Decimal System numbers and categories for each team. (See page 37 for this list.)
- lists of book titles

PROCEDURE
   1. Prepare the game sheets. Every time a new game is played, a new game sheet is required for each team.
   2. Prepare lists of 10 book titles. A new list is needed for each game.
   3. Decide how you wish to present the book title lists — on the chalkboard, on chart paper, or on an overhead projector — and prepare them accordingly.
   4. Divide your group into teams.
   5. Explain the rules:
      a. The object of the game is to be the first team to complete a correct list of book titles according to the Dewey Decimal System.
      b. The first player writes a title from the master list next to the correct category and then passes the game sheet and pencil to the next player.
      c. The second player must write a different title next to a different category, and so on.
      d. If a player finds an error made by a team member, the player may correct it.
      e. The last player stands when finished.
   6. Give the first player on each team a game sheet and a pencil, reveal the book title list, and give the signal to start.

Where Is It?

A. Nonfiction: Which topics are represented by these Dewey Decimal System numbers?

1. 000–099 _____

2. 100–199 _____

3. 200–299 _____

4. 300–399 _____

5. 400–499 _____

6. 500–599 _____

7. 600–699 _____

8. 700–799 _____

9. 800–899 _____

10. 900–999 _____

B. Fiction: Number the books below in the order in which they would be arranged in a library.

____ *Benjy Goes to Town,* by Sara Jackson

____ *Benjy Finds a Thief,* by Sara Jackson

____ *Ben and His Motorcycle,* by Anne Adamson

____ *Betsy Buys a Bike,* by John Callahan

____ *Albert Is Always Late,* by Alan Waters

Following Leads

In detective work, a lead is a clue. The Dewey Decimal System can give you leads to interesting reading by telling you where to find topics in the library. Here are some facts about the Dewey Decimal System:

1. The system groups nonfiction books by topic.
2. Each topic has a number.
3. Fiction books are arranged by the author's last name.
4. Each book has a call number that is its "address" in the library.

Browse through each Dewey Decimal System section in your library. Look for leads and follow them to interesting books. Find a book that interests you in each section. Fill in the chart below so that you can find the book quickly when you want to read it.

Section	Call Number	Title and Author
000 – 099	_____	_____
100 – 199	_____	_____
200 – 299	_____	_____
300 – 399	_____	_____
400 – 499	_____	_____
500 – 599	_____	_____
600 – 699	_____	_____
700 – 799	_____	_____
800 – 899	_____	_____
900 – 999	_____	_____
Fiction A – H	_____	_____
Fiction I – O	_____	_____
Fiction P – Z	_____	_____

Good detectives check out their leads! Follow up your leads by reading the books you listed.

Looking for Clues

Knowing where items belong will help you find clues. Read the Dewey Decimal System classification chart below. Then read the title of each book listed below. Decide which Dewey Decimal System category each book belongs to. Write the number of the category in the blank.

Dewey Decimal System Classification Numbers

000–099 General Works (encyclopedias, references)
100–199 Philosophy (ideas about behavior, thought, knowledge, nature, and psychology)
200–299 Religion (all religions of all time)
300–399 Social Sciences (education, law, civics)
400–499 Language (languages, grammar, etymology)
500–599 Pure Science (biology, chemistry, physics)
600–699 Technology (applied science, home, industry)
700–799 Arts (music, painting, sculpture, games)
800–899 Literature (poetry, plays, and books about literature)
900–999 History (biography, geography, history of civilizations)

_____ 1. *Story of the Alphabet,* by Edward Clodd

_____ 2. *Life in Colonial America,* by Edith Speare

_____ 3. *Roads,* by Jon W. Boardman

_____ 4. *All About Stars,* by Anne T. White

_____ 5. *The First Book of the Olympic Games,* by John Welsh

_____ 6. *Laughable Limericks,* by Sara and John E. Brown

_____ 7. *The First Book of the Constitution,* by R. B. Norris

_____ 8. *Skateboarding,* by Howart Reiser

_____ 9. *The Magic of Music,* by Lorrain E. Watters

_____ 10. *Familiar Quotations,* by John Bartlett

_____ 11. *Gods and Heroes,* by Sally Benson

_____ 12. *The Republic,* by Plato

The Dewey Decimal System 37

Remembering the Clues

An easy way to remember facts is to make a *mnemonic* device — something to help you remember. For example, you can use the first letters of the facts you want to remember as the first letters of the words in a sentence. Do you know the names of the lines of the G clef in music? They are: "Every good boy does fine" — e, g, b, d, f.

A. Suppose you need to remember the planets in order of increasing size. They are: Mercury, Pluto, Mars, Venus, Earth, Neptune, Uranus, Saturn, and Jupiter. Use the first letter of each planet's name to complete the mnemonic sentence below.

___echanics ___repare ___any ___enus ___xpeditions,

___ever ___sing ___trange ___alopies.

B. Try making your own mnemonic device to help you remember the Dewey Decimal System categories in order. The categories are: General, Philosophy, Religion, Social Sciences, Language, Science, Technology, Arts, Literature, and History. Write your words in the blanks below. Then write out your complete mnemonic sentence.

g_____ p_____ r_____

s_____ l_____ s_____

t_____ a_____ l_____

h_____

_____

_____

_____

Dewey Decimal System Test

Match each book title below with the Dewey Decimal System category it belongs in. Write the first number of the category in the blank next to the title.

Dewey Decimal System

000 – 099	General Works	500 – 599	Pure Science
100 – 199	Philosophy	600 – 699	Technology
200 – 299	Religion	700 – 799	Arts
300 – 399	Social Sciences	800 – 899	Literature
400 – 499	Language	900 – 999	History

Book Titles

_____ 1. *The History of New York City*

_____ 2. *French for Beginners*

_____ 3. *New Games for Large Groups*

_____ 4. *Hinduism, the Ancient Religion*

_____ 5. *Being and Nothingness*

_____ 6. *All About Computers*

_____ 7. *The Scientific Dictionary*

_____ 8. *Poems to Make You Laugh*

_____ 9. *The Art of the Navahos*

_____ 10. *Paul Revere Rides Again*

The Card Catalog

Objective

The students will become familiar with the card catalog and the three types of information cards used in a card catalog.

Suggestions for Use

The ability to use the card catalog efficiently makes finding a book much easier. Periodically review the skills in this section, since they are probably the most useful to library users.

Motivational Riddle
It's in the Cards

SUGGESTION FOR USE Use this riddle to stimulate interest in the card catalog. Attach the riddle to the magnifying glass in the Booksnoop poster. Challenge your students to make up their own riddles that can be answered with a book title.

RIDDLE

A nonfiction book I am, that is true.
To find me is the thing you must do.
Mischievous I am, my title does say.
I'm about a raccoon that likes to play.
A direction is my author's last name.
Sure hope you can find me and win the game!
Answer: Rascal, by Sterling North

Bulletin Board
Catalog These Bees

DESCRIPTION The students will sort catalog cards by type—author, subject, or title.

MATERIALS
- construction paper, brown and yellow
- tagboard, brown and yellow
- black felt-tip pen
- stapler
- hole punch
- pushpins
- discarded library catalog cards from the *B*s or blank index cards to make your own

PROCEDURE

1. Prepare the caption Catalog These Bees, then staple it in position on the bulletin board.

2. Make three beehives from yellow or light brown construction paper. Label them Subject, Author, and Title.

3. Use yellow tagboard and a black felt-tip pen to make a bee for each catalog card you have collected or made.

4. Staple each catalog card to the body of a bee. Punch a hole in the top of each bee (avoiding the printing on the card). The hole must be large enough to accommodate the head of a pushpin.

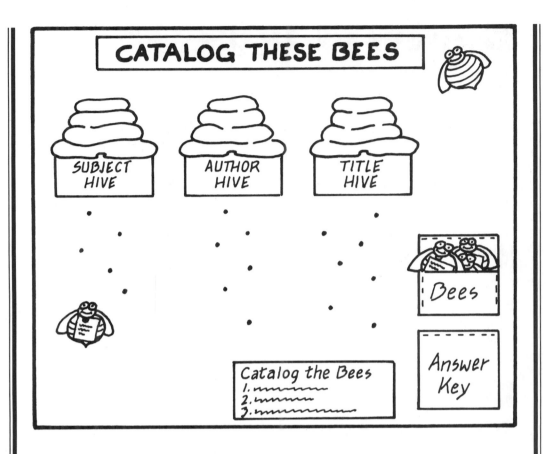

5. Make a storage pocket for the bees. Fold a piece of construction paper up one third. Staple the outside edges to form a pocket.

6. Print an answer key on a piece of construction paper. Cover it with another piece of construction paper labeled Answer Key, and staple it at the top to make a flap.

7. Print the following directions on a piece of construction paper:

Catalog These Bees

1. Put the catalog cards in the correct hives.
2. Lift the flap to check your answers.
3. Return the bees to the storage pocket when finished.

8. Staple the components in position on the bulletin board. Place the number of pushpins needed for each type of card beneath each hive. The cards rest on the plastic part of the pushpin.

Game
Card Catalog Fish

OBJECTIVE The students will match the author, title, and subject cards for a book.

DESCRIPTION The familiar game of "Go Fish" makes matching the author, title, and subject cards an enjoyable way to learn to recognize the three types of cards.

MATERIALS

- 51 blank cards cut to playing card size *or* 17 sets of discarded catalog cards

PROCEDURE

1. Prepare the playing cards. If your librarian does not have old cards to give you, print author, title, and subject cards for 17 books.

2. Place a copy of the following game directions at the game table:

Card Catalog Fish

1. Two to six people may play.
2. The cards are shuffled, and six cards are dealt to each player.
3. The remaining cards are placed face down in the center of the table.
4. The player on the right of the dealer goes first.
5. The player asks the person on the right for an author, subject, or title card but does not specify for which book. If the player on the right has the kind of card requested, he or she must surrender it. If the player does not have the requested card, a card is drawn from the pile. Play moves to the right.
6. When all three cards for a book are collected, the player lays them down and gets an extra turn.
7. The player who makes the most sets of three cards is the winner.

3. Increase the difficulty of the game by using cards featuring the same subject or similar titles.

Tracing the Cards

Use the information below to make three catalog cards for the book.

Winning at Tennis   Brownsville Publishers 1982   176p illus.   Erica Gonzales   Illus by Janet Winslow.   786 G   TENNIS

1.

Type of card: _____

2.

Type of card: _____

3.

Type of card: _____

Tracing the Trays

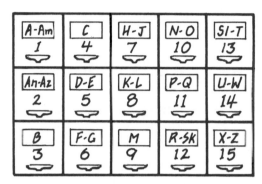

A. For each book below, write the number of the catalog card tray above that would hold the title card for the book.

_____ 1. *What Animal Is It?,* by Anna Pretorius

_____ 2. *All About Birds,* by Robert Lemmon

_____ 3. *A Midsummer Night's Dream,* by William Shakespeare

_____ 4. *Adventures with the Heroes,* by Catherine F. Sellew

_____ 5. *The Buildings of Ancient Egypt,* by Helen Leacroft

B. For each book below, write the number of the catalog card tray above that would hold the subject card for the book.

_____ 1. *Carlsbad Caverns*   _____ 5. *Treaty of Utrecht*

_____ 2. *Malaria*   _____ 6. *Seashells*

_____ 3. *Hundred Years' War*   _____ 7. *Map Making*

_____ 4. *Sir Lancelot*   _____ 8. *Rodents*

C. For each book below, write the number of the catalog card tray above that would hold the author card for the book.

_____ 1. *The Susquehanna from New York to Chesapeake,* by Elizabeth Carmer

_____ 2. *Sixth Sense,* by Larry Kettlekamp

_____ 3. *Rip Van Winkle and the Legend of Sleepy Hollow,* by Washington Irving

_____ 4. *My Village in Greece,* by Sonia and Tim Gidel

_____ 5. *White Horses and Black Bulls,* by Alan C. Jenkins

Clues in the Trays

A. Explore any card catalog tray. Use the tray to complete each sentence below.

1. My tray number is _____ .

2. It contains entries beginning with _____ and ending

   with _____ .

3. Four guide words used in this tray are _____ ,

   _____ , _____ , and _____ .

B. Follow the instructions to answer each question below.

1. Find an author card. What information is on the first line of the card?

   _____

   How many books by that author are indexed in your catalog

   tray? _____

2. Find a title card for a fiction book. What is the title of the book?

   _____

3. Find a title card for a nonfiction book. What is the title of the book?

   _____

4. Find two titles that begin with the same word. What are the titles?

   _____ and _____

5. Find cards for two nonfiction books. What are the call numbers?

   _____ and _____

6. Find a subject card. What is the heading on the card?

   _____ . How many books are listed under this

   heading? _____

Clues in the Cards

A. Use this catalog card to answer the questions below.

```
636.7    DOGS
  Mc     McCloy, James
              Dogs at work.   Illus by Sheila Beatty.
           Crown 1979        74p illus.
```

1. Type of card? _____

2. What is the book's call number? _____

3. What part of the call number identifies the author? _____

B. Use this catalog card to answer the questions below.

```
293
  C      Closse, Robert
              Odin and his family.   Illus by Betty Clark.
           Crisfield Publishers 1970    120p illus.
```

1. Type of card? _____

2. What is the title of the book? _____

3. Who wrote the book? _____

C. Use this catalog card to answer the questions below.

```
           Mystery at lochearn hill
           Kasner, Lawrence
              Mystery at lochern hill.   Illus by George Knobb.
           Scoson Publishers 1972    94p illus.
```

1. Type of card? _____

2. Where in the library would you find the book? _____

3. Who drew the pictures for the book? _____

Unscramble the Clues

Use the "clues" below to make three catalog cards for the book.

Life in ancient egypt   Scribner Publishers 1975
164p illus.   Illus by Marg. Boehmer.
Kenneth Fowler   932 F
EGYPT

1. Subject card

```
        _____

  __    _____

        _____

        _____
```

2. Title card

```
        _____

  __    _____

        _____

        _____
```

3. Author card

```
  __    _____

        _____

        _____
```

Card Catalog Test

A. Name the three types of cards in a card catalog.

_____ _____ _____

B. Use this catalog card to answer the questions below.

AMERICAN HISTORY

976.6
A   Abbott, Sarah H.

     The gold rush days.   Illus by Jane Soo.

Goldstone 1965   172p illus.

---

1. What is the title of the book? _____

2. Who is the author? _____

3. When was the book copyrighted? _____

4. What is its call number? _____

5. Who is the publisher? _____

C. Use the information below to make a title card for the book.

Mystery of the missing computer   138p illus.
Nancy Morrison   Weldon Publishing 1983
Illus by Jerry Smith.

_____

_____

_____

_____

Unit 5

The Thesaurus

Objective

The students will use a thesaurus to find synonyms for given words and will learn its value as a tool for better writing.

Suggestions for Use

Everyone will benefit from browsing through a thesaurus. Challenge your more able students to find more than one substitute word. Encourage students to share interesting words they find. Make charts of words that can be substituted for those overworked words you are so tired of reading in compositions: *nice, happy, beautiful, good,* and so forth.

Motivational Riddle
One to Nine

SUGGESTIONS FOR USE Use this riddle after you have introduced the thesaurus. Attach the riddle to the magnifying glass in the Booksnoop poster. Encourage your students to make up riddles of their own that follow this pattern.

RIDDLE

My first is in <u>lame</u>, but not in <u>pale</u>.
With my second and fourth you can see my third and fifth.
My third is in <u>name</u>, but not in <u>game</u>.
My fifth is like a snake.
My sixth is one hundred.
My seventh falls between <u>t</u> and <u>v</u>.
Although I have an eighth and ninth,
No further clues will I give you.
Just look in your thesaurus under *small*,
And you will know the name to call!
   Answer: Miniscule

Bulletin Board
Theo Saurus

OBJECTIVE The students will use the thesaurus to find synonyms for overworked words.

DESCRIPTION Our favorite dinosaur, Theo Saurus, asks your students to change his spots by finding new words for those worn-out favorites.

MATERIALS
- construction paper, three or more colors
- felt-tip pen
- stapler
- scissors
- ditto master
- compass or saucer

PROCEDURE

1. Make Theo Saurus from construction paper. Staple him in position on the bulletin board.

2. Prepare the caption and print the speech balloon, using construction paper for both. Staple them in position on the bulletin board.

3. Using a saucer or a compass, make a ditto master for Theo's spots. Print Name and Old Word on one circle and New Word on another. Run the ditto master on construction paper and cut out the circles.

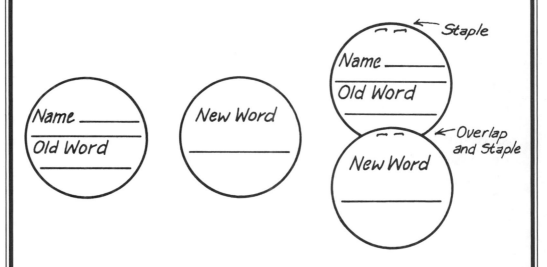

4. Make a storage pocket by folding a piece of construction paper up one third and stapling along the edges. Label the pocket New Spots and staple it in position on the bulletin board. Place the new-word spots and a felt-tip pen in the pocket. Make another pocket, labeled Old Spots. Place the old-word spots and a felt-tip pen inside.

5. Cut out six more circles and print an overused word on each one. Position the circles on Theo.

6. Print the following directions on a piece of construction paper. Then staple the paper in position on the bulletin board.

Change Theo's Spots

1. Find a word on Theo that you use too often when you write.
2. Use the thesaurus to find an interesting synonym for your overused word.
3. Take an old spot and a new spot and fill in the blanks.
4. Show your new spot to your teacher and ask for the stapler. Staple your new spot to the board so that it overlaps the old spot.

Game
Do You Understand?

OBJECTIVE The students will use the thesaurus to rewrite familiar material.

DESCRIPTION Teams compete to stump each other with translations of familiar sayings and titles.

MATERIALS

- at least one thesaurus for each team
- game list for each team

PROCEDURE

1. Prepare the game lists, each with five titles or sayings. For example, use five television show titles, five book titles, five song titles, or five proverbs.

2. Divide your group into three or more teams.

3. Explain the rules of the game:
   a. The object of the game is to earn the most points by preparing the translations and using them to stump the other teams.
   b. Each team will be given a game sheet.
   c. Use the thesaurus to translate the material on the game sheet. (*Read the examples below.*) The first team to complete the translations earns five points, the second earns three points, and the third, one point. (*Adjust the scoring if you have more than three teams.*)
   d. Each team will challenge the others to guess the original material.
   e. Each time you stump another team, your team will earn a point.

EXAMPLES

1. "Birds of a feather flock together" becomes "Fowl of similar plumage congregate collectively."

2. "Star Wars" becomes "Conflict Among the Celestial Bodies."

3. "Rock Around the Clock" becomes "Circular Transit About the Chronograph."

Crime Stopper

The thesaurus, or dictionary of synonyms, is a crime stopper. It will help you avoid the crime of using the same old words over and over. Read this sample index from a thesaurus.

shock, *v.* surprise 407
   upset 692
   repel 579, 617
shocking horrible 694
   harmful 904
   fearful 355
   hateful *721*
   unsavory 668
shoe *590*

Here is what you would find when you turned to entry #590 to find another word for *shoe*.

590. **CLOTHING.** — *N.* **clothing,** covering, garment, costume, attire, vestment.
   outfit, uniform, suit, gear, equipment.
   dress, suit, evening clothes, tuxedo.
   cloak, cape, mantle, shawl.
   jacket, vest, waistcoat.
   headdress, hat, sombrero, cap, bonnet.
   shoe, slipper, moccasin, sneaker, sandal, galosh, clog, snowshoe, ski, Oxford, patent leather.

Sailing by Thesaurus

A. A thesaurus will help you sail through your writing assignments by helping you find interesting words. Use the index to find the key word *good*. Find the list of synonyms for *good*. List three synonyms for *good* that you think are interesting.

_____   _____   _____

B. Use your thesaurus to find a word to replace each underlined word in the paragraph below. Write each replacement word and the entry word or key word that helped you find the replacement.

Sailing in Olden Times

The men who volunteered for an (1) ocean trip in the sailing ships of the 1700s really earned their (2) pay. They had to (3) fight the (4) unfriendly wind and weather. The ship might be (5) sunk by a storm of (6) great (7) strength. Often a ship remained (8) motionless for days. As a (9) result, the trip would be (10) lengthened by many days.

Replacement Words	Entry or Key Words
1. _____	_____
2. _____	_____
3. _____	_____
4. _____	_____
5. _____	_____
6. _____	_____
7. _____	_____
8. _____	_____
9. _____	_____
10. _____	_____

Find the Rhyme for Us Using a Thesaurus

Use your thesaurus to find synonyms for the words below. Each clue is a word that rhymes with the answer you will find in the thesaurus.

Words	Clues	Synonyms
1. cripple	name	_____
2. hate	restore	_____
3. crash	subside	_____
4. talkative	vivacious	_____
5. conquer	renew	_____
6. favorable	malicious	_____
7. distort	marble	_____
8. strength	bigger	_____
9. evil	minister	_____
10. lie in wait	clerk	_____
11. counterfeit	lamb	_____
12. idea	lotion	_____
13. explore	robe	_____
14. attention	speed	_____
15. search	rest	_____
16. regret	endorse	_____
17. enemy	low	_____
18. lean and lanky	taunt	_____
19. color	do	_____

The Thesaurus Goes to the Movies

Light, sound, and motion make a movie special. Use your thesaurus to put each word in the box below into the correct category. If your thesaurus has a Synopsis of Categories section in the front, use it.

Light	Sound	Motion
_____	_____	_____
_____	_____	_____
_____	_____	_____
_____	_____	_____
_____	_____	_____
_____	_____	_____
_____	_____	_____
_____	_____	_____
_____	_____	_____
_____	_____	_____
_____	_____	_____
_____	_____	_____
_____	_____	_____

Word Box

acoustics, activity, actuation, budge, dynamic, emanation, flow, fluorescent, flux, gleam, glimmer, glint, glow, illumination, intonation, kinesis, lucence, luminary, luminescence, luminous, luster, mobilization, monotone, motor, movableness, movement, noise, ongoing, pitch, radiance, report, sheen, sonance, sonic, soniferous, stir, timbre, tonality, tonation, tone, tonic, travel

Thesaurus Test

A. Read the statements below. Write *true* or *false* next to each one.

_____ 1. A thesaurus lists antonyms under every key word.

_____ 2. A thesaurus will help you pronounce a word correctly.

_____ 3. A thesaurus will help you choose a synonym for a word.

_____ 4. All the words in a dictionary are in a thesaurus.

_____ 5. A thesaurus will help you find words to make your writing more interesting.

B. Use your thesaurus. Rewrite the sentences below using a synonym for each underlined word.

1. Isn't a molecule <u>small</u>? _____

2. The <u>house</u> was on a street. _____

3. The sunset was <u>pretty</u>. _____

4. He <u>walked</u> away <u>quickly</u>. _____

C. Use your thesaurus. Write three synonyms for each word below.

1. story _____ _____ _____

2. friend _____ _____ _____

3. old _____ _____ _____

4. said _____ _____ _____

5. want _____ _____ _____

6. hot _____ _____ _____

7. look _____ _____ _____

8. happy _____ _____ _____

Unit 6

The Atlas

Objective

The students will become familiar with the structure of an atlas and with its values and limitations.

Suggestions for Use

Map-reading skills are not taught in this unit. This unit will make the atlas a friendly book for your students, one they will feel comfortable using because they know where to look to locate information. These activities can be reused when the group progresses to more complete and complex atlases.

Motivational Riddle
Exploring

SUGGESTIONS FOR USE Use this riddle as the conclusion to your introductory lesson. Attach the riddle to the magnifying glass in the Booksnoop poster. Then have your students choose countries and write their own "exploring" riddles for presentation to the class the following day.

RIDDLE
South of the United States, but north of Argentina.
Southeast of Japan, but northeast of Australia.
West of Venezuela, but north of Ecuador and Peru.
South of Panama, and named for a famous explorer of 1492.
Your atlas will reveal my name to you!
   Answer: Colombia

Bulletin Board
Atlas Match

OBJECTIVE The students will use an atlas to match cities with states.

DESCRIPTION Provide the names of cities and states you wish to be matched. The students match each city with its state by placing the city next to the name of its state. This board can be updated easily by changing the matches.

MATERIALS
- tagboard
- construction paper
- pen
- scissors
- pushpins
- hole punch
- compass or circle patterns

PROCEDURE
1. Decide how many matches you have space for on the bulletin board. Make a list of names of cities and states you want the students to match.
2. Cut five large circles from tagboard. Print one letter of the word *ATLAS* on each circle. Arrange the circles in order vertically on the bulletin board and staple them in place.

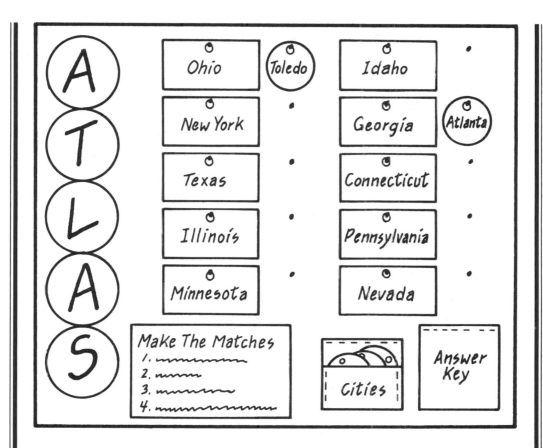

The following diagram shows a bulletin board with the word ATLAS spelled vertically in circles. State name rectangles are labeled: Ohio, New York, Texas, Illinois, Minnesota, Idaho, Georgia, Connecticut, Pennsylvania, Nevada. City circles labeled Toledo and Atlanta. A "Make The Matches" list (numbered 1-4), a "Cities" pocket, and an "Answer Key" box appear at the bottom.

3. Cut a smaller circle from tagboard for each city on your match list. Punch a hole large enough to accommodate the head of a pushpin about 1 inch from the outer edge of each circle. Print a city name on each circle.

4. Cut rectangles from tagboard. Print a state name on each rectangle. Staple the rectangles in position on the bulletin board. Place a pushpin next to each state name.

5. Make a storage pocket by folding a piece of construction paper up one third and stapling along the edges. Label the pocket Cities. Staple the pocket in position on the bulletin board. Place the city name circles in the pocket.

6. Place an atlas at the bulletin board.

7. Print the following directions on a piece of construction paper. Staple it in position on the bulletin board.

Make the Matches
1. Take the circles from the pocket.
2. Match each city with its state by hanging it beside its state.
3. Check your answers by using the atlas index.
4. Return the cities to the pocket when finished.

8. Update this bulletin board by changing the city names.

Game

Westward, Ho!

OBJECTIVE The students will trace a westward route across the United States using maps in an atlas.

DESCRIPTION Relay teams compete to be the first to complete a map route through capital cities across the United States to reach a given destination.

MATERIALS

- atlas for each team
- piece of paper and pencil for each team

PROCEDURE

1. Pick a capital city on the east coast as a starting point and a capital city on the west coast as a destination. Write these city names on the chalkboard.

2. Divide your group into teams of three to five players each.

3. Explain the rules:

   a. The object of the game is to be the first team to reach the city of destination using the atlas to plan the route.

   b. The first player uses the atlas to find the location of the starting city. Then the player "travels" to a bordering state and writes the name of its capital city on the game sheet. The game sheet, pencil, and closed atlas is passed to the next player.

   c. The second player finds the state capital listed by the first player, "travels" to a bordering state, and writes the name of its capital city. The game sheet, pencil, and closed atlas are passed to the third player.

   d. The player who reaches the destination writes the city's name, stands up, and says, "Westward, ho!"

   e. When all teams have finished, the routes will be checked for accuracy against a wall map. The first team with a correct route is the winner.

VARIATIONS

1. Increase the level of difficulty by restricting travel to cities of a certain population size.

2. Travel around the world using the capitals of countries.

Your Travel Guide: The Atlas

The atlas has two sections that will help you in your travels: the table of contents and the index. Read the examples of these sections below.

Contents

Index

Getting Acquainted

Get to know your atlas. Explore the table of contents and any other lists of maps that are in your atlas.

A. Write the number of the page on which you will find each map listed below. There may be more than one page number for a map.

Map	Page
1. Political divisions of the world	_____
2. Physical map of the world	_____
3. Climates of the world	_____
4. Temperatures of the world	_____
5. Rainfall of the world	_____
6. Ocean currents of the world	_____
7. Natural vegetation of the world	_____
8. Soil groups of the world	_____
9. Population of the world	_____
10. Agricultural products of the world	_____
11. Mineral deposits of the world	_____
12. Languages of the world	_____
13. Religions of the world	_____

B. Some atlases have interesting lists—for example, of the world's longest rivers, highest mountains, and largest cities—in the back. Look in the back of your atlas just before the index. Write the names of the other lists you find.

_____

_____

Making Conversation

A. Find the index in your atlas. Locate the entry for each city listed below. Tell the latitude and longitude for each city (if the index lists it) and the page on which you will find it.

City	Lat.	Long.	Page
1. Athens, Greece	_____	_____	_____
2. Bern, Switzerland	_____	_____	_____
3. Cairo, Egypt	_____	_____	_____
4. Toronto, Canada	_____	_____	_____
5. Washington, D.C., U.S.A.	_____	_____	_____
6. Mexico City, Mexico	_____	_____	_____
7. La Paz, Bolivia	_____	_____	_____
8. Sydney, Australia	_____	_____	_____
9. Calcutta, India	_____	_____	_____
10. Seoul, Korea	_____	_____	_____
11. Baghdad, Iraq	_____	_____	_____
12. Mandalay, Burma	_____	_____	_____
13. Ankara, Turkey	_____	_____	_____
14. Caracas, Venezuela	_____	_____	_____
15. Nairobi, Kenya	_____	_____	_____

B. List the names of three other cities that interest you, and complete the table for them.

1. _____ _____ _____ _____

2. _____ _____ _____ _____

3. _____ _____ _____ _____

Being Neighborly

Use the table of contents in your atlas to find the maps showing the countries listed below. Write the page number for each one. Turn to the map and find the country's neighbors. Write the names of at least two neighboring countries for each country below.

Country	Page	Neighbors
1. France	_____	_____
		_____
2. Sweden	_____	_____
		_____
3. Hungary	_____	_____
		_____
4. Libya	_____	_____
		_____
5. Iraq	_____	_____
		_____
6. El Salvador	_____	_____
		_____
7. Bolivia	_____	_____
		_____
8. India	_____	_____
		_____
9. Mexico	_____	_____
		_____

Atlas Test

A. Place a check beside each statement below that is true for your atlas.

___ 1. My atlas has an index of place names.

___ 2. My atlas tells how to pronounce unusual names.

___ 3. My atlas has a table of contents listing the types of maps.

___ 4. My atlas lists the capital cities of the world.

___ 5. My atlas shows the physical features of Mars.

___ 6. My atlas shows the farm products of the world.

___ 7. My atlas helps me spell tricky words.

___ 8. My atlas tells about important explorers.

___ 9. My atlas lists the largest mountains of the world.

___ 10. My atlas lists most of the rivers of the world.

B. Number the entries in each group below in the order in which you would find them in the index of an atlas.

1. ___ New Haven   2. ___ Lancaster

    ___ N. Park   ___ L. San Marcos

    ___ Nile River   ___ Los Altos

    ___ Northfield   ___ Lincoln

    ___ New Windsor   ___ Le Grand

Unit 7

Bartlett's Familiar Quotations

Objective

The students will learn to use *Familiar Quotations,* by John Bartlett.

Before You Begin

Browse through Bartlett's yourself and have some fun finding the origin of the sayings we hear and use every day. If the *Oxford Dictionary of Quotations* is available, compare its contents and structure with Bartlett's. Plan to have your more able students make these comparisons, too.

Motivational Riddle
Meet Mr. Bartlett

SUGGESTIONS FOR USE Use this riddle to introduce your students to Bartlett's *Familiar Quotations*. (The *Oxford Dictionary of Quotations* does not contain the riddle's quotations.) Attach the riddle to the magnifying glass in the Booksnoop poster. After this riddle has been solved, have your students print their favorite quotations to be put on the poster. Have the student who finds the author supply the next quotation.

RIDDLE

Can you tell me who was the one
Who said these words? You'll have fun!
"Little strokes fell great oaks."
Here's another clue, folks:
"An empty bag cannot stand upright."
With these clues, whom do you cite?
One more clue, then I'll cease.
Who said, "There never was a good war or a bad peace"?
  Answer: Benjamin Franklin

Bulletin Board
Match the Pears

OBJECTIVE The students will use *Familiar Quotations* to match quotations with authors.

DESCRIPTION Quotations are written on sentence strips, and the authors' names are printed on pears. The students use *Familiar Quotations* to make the matches.

MATERIALS
- five sheets of yellow tagboard
- sentence strips
- pen
- stapler
- pushpins
- hole punch

PROCEDURE

1. Choose the quotations you wish to use. Print each quotation on a sentence strip. Write the author's name on the back for your reference.

2. Cut two large pears from yellow tagboard and print MATCH THE on one and USE BARTLETT'S on the other. Staple them in position on the bulletin board.

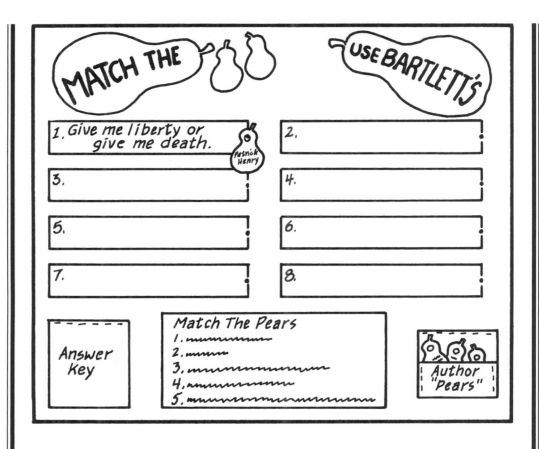

3. Cut out smaller pears. You will need a small pear for each quotation and two more to complete the caption. Position the two caption pears next to the MATCH THE pear and staple it to the board.

4. Print an author's name on each of the remaining pears. Punch a hole in the stem end of each pear. The hole must be large enough to allow the pear to be suspended from a pushpin.

5. Arrange the sentence strips as shown in the illustration. Place a pushpin at the end of each sentence strip.

6. Print an answer key and staple it to the bulletin board. Cover the key with a piece of paper stapled at the top to make a flap. Label it Answer Key.

7. Make a storage pocket for the author pears by folding up the bottom third of a piece of paper and stapling the edges. Staple the pocket to the bulletin board.

8. Print the following directions on a piece of paper and staple it to the bulletin board.

Match the Pears

1. Read the quotations.
2. Take the author's name pears from the pocket.
3. Use Bartlett's to find the author of each quotation.
4. Hang the author's name beside his or her quote.
5. Check the answer key and return the pears to the pocket when finished.

Game
Bart-ades

OBJECTIVE The students will use Bartlett's to find quotations.

DESCRIPTION Adapt the familiar game of Charades to provide an enjoyable break for your students. Allow time for the students to find quotations to contribute to the game.

MATERIALS
- Bartlett's *Familiar Quotations*
- slip of paper and pen for each player
- shoe box

PROCEDURE

1. Plan ahead for this game. Several days in advance, have each participant find a quotation in Bartlett's that can be pantomimed. Direct them to copy the quotation and its author's name on a slip of paper and place it in the box.

2. On the day of the game, explain the rules:
- a. The object of the game is to be the first to say the quotation correctly.
- b. The first player begins the game by drawing a slip from the box.
- c. The player reads the slip silently, announces its author, and then pantomimes the quote.
- d. The other players will guess the words as they are pantomimed.
- e. When all the words have been pantomimed, the player calls on students to say the entire quotation.
- f. The first student to say it correctly draws the next slip.
- g. The player who contributed the quotation watches as the group plays.

VARIATION
Play Bart-ades in teams. Each team prepares a list of quotations for the other team to pantomime and guess.

Meet Mr. Bartlett

Below is part of an index of the type used by Mr. Bartlett in compiling his book.

Happy and sad, 672
   as a clam, 325
   as kings, 478
   as the grass was green, 905
   consider, and the, 342
   goes as lucky goes, 660
   never so, as we suppose, 512
   the man whose wish, 596

Below is an example of an entry in Bartlett's *Familiar Quotations.*

ARTHUR GUITERMAN
(1871–1943)

Oh, the saddest of sights in a world of sin
Is a little lost pup with his tail tucked in!
Little Lost Pup, Stanza 1

He stood with his muzzle thrust out through the door
The whole forty days of that terrible pour!
Because of which drenching, the Sages unfold,
The Nose of a Healthy Dog always is Cold.[1]
The Dog's Cold Nose

[1]Most frozen was his honest nose,
And never could it lose again
The dampness of that dreadful rain.
MARGARET EYTINGE,
Why the Dog's Nose Is Cold

Getting in Step with Bartlett

Bartlett's has two indexes: an index of authors and an index of quotations. All entries are alphabetical. To find a quotation, you need to find its key word first. The key words of some quotations are listed below, along with their key lines. Number each group of key lines in the order in which they would appear in the index.

1. fields

____ babbled of green

____ of air

____ and the gliding streams

____ boundless and beautiful

____ and the waters shout

2. cat

____ so sweet a

____ bell the

____ nine lives like a

____ feet, fog comes on little

____ in the pan

3. city

____ is greater than its bricks

____ in the sea

____ is historic

____ is the teacher of man

____ is not builded in a day

4. friend

____ in need

____ dog is man's best

____ faithful is the best

____ equal to a brother

____ who deserts you

Who Said That?

Read each quotation below. Circle the key word that will help you find each quotation in the index of lines in Bartlett's. Then find each quotation and write the name of the person who said it.

1. All that we see or seem

   Is but a dream within a dream. _____

2. An' the Gobble-uns 'at gits you

   Ef you

   Don't

   Watch

   Out! _____

3. It is not only fine feathers that make fine birds.

   _____

4. Time is but the stream I go a-fishing in._____

5. As idle as a painted ship

   Upon a painted ocean. _____

6. In love of home, the love of country has its rise.

   _____

7. To be great is to be misunderstood. _____

8. A sharp tongue is the only edge tool that grows keener with

   constant use. _____

9. I think that I shall never see

   A poem lovely as a tree. _____

10. I think that I shall never see

    A billboard lovely as a tree.

    Indeed, unless the billboards fall,

    I'll never see a tree at all. _____

I. M. A. Booksnoop reproducible page, copyright © 1983

The Case of the Interrupted Quotation

Someone has been playing tricks with your tape recorder! Use Bartlett's to find the missing line or lines of each quotation below. Circle the key word that will help you find each line in the index. Then find the quotation and complete the sentence or stanza.

1. One if by land, _____

_____

_____

_____

2. Fifteen men on the Dead Man's Chest—

_____

_____

_____

3. Tiger! tiger! burning bright

_____

_____

_____

4. Has thou named all the birds without a gun?

_____

_____

5. To err is human, _____

6. O Captain! my Captain! _____

_____

_____

Bartlett's Test

A. Read each sentence below. Write *true* or *false* next to each one.

_____ 1. Bartlett's index is arranged alphabetically by key words from the quotations.

_____ 2. All the writings or sayings of a famous person are recorded in Bartlett's.

_____ 3. There is a table of contents in Bartlett's.

_____ 4. Only Americans are quoted in Bartlett's.

_____ 5. Bartlett's lists only quotations that are less than 100 years old.

B. Circle the key word or words that would help you find each quotation below.

1. They also serve who only stand and wait.
2. Some books are to be tasted, others to be swallowed, and some few to be chewed and digested.
3. For fools rush in where angels fear to tread.
4. Happy is the house that shelters a friend.
5. Three may keep a secret, if two of them are dead.
6. The reward of a thing well done, is to have done it.
7. Rose is a rose is a rose is a rose.
8. Something there is that doesn't love a wall.
9. It's all in the day's work.
10. If wishes were horses, beggars might ride.

Unit 8

The Almanac

Objective

The students will become familiar with the almanac and the many types of information it presents.

Before You Begin

Gather as many almanacs as you can. Almanacs do not have to be up-to-date to provide the type of practice the students need to learn to use an almanac.

Motivational Riddle
Department Store for Questioners

SUGGESTIONS FOR USE Use this riddle to encourage your students to dig into the almanac. Fill in the blanks in the riddle to correspond to the facts you choose from your almanacs. Attach the riddle to the magnifying glass in the Booksnoop poster. After the riddle has been solved, have your students find their own facts. Substitute the students' questions for lines five through eight.

RIDDLE

The almanac is a great book to read!
In it are facts to fill every need.
Here are some questions, the answers to which
You'll find in the almanac—it's a cinch!
In 19____ what male actor won the Oscar?
In the Olympic shot put, who was the star?
From _____ to _____ is how many miles?
How many tornadoes in the weather files?
You'll find all those answers and many more,
In the almanac, the book department store!
  Answer: Use your almanac to determine the correct answers.

Bulletin Board
Elapsed Events

OBJECTIVE The students will use the almanac to find events that occurred on given dates.

DESCRIPTION The students will complete the bulletin board by finding events that match the dates of the calendar you prepare. The almanac search that results will familiarize your students with the myriad information available in an almanac.

MATERIALS

- bulletin board backing paper, approximately 2 feet by 3 feet
- construction paper
- pen
- meter stick
- stapler
- almanacs

BOOKSNOOP'S ELAPSED EVENTS MONTH

	1	2	3	4	5	6
7	8	9	10	11	12	13
14	15	16	17	18	19	20
21	22	23	24	25	26	27
28	29	30	31			

PROCEDURE

1. Prepare a calendar grid for a month of your choice on backing paper. Number the days in the top left corners of the grid spaces. Staple the grid to the bulletin board.

2. Use the overhead projection method to reproduce the picture of I. M. A. Booksnoop (see page 1). Staple the picture to the bulletin board.

3. Prepare the caption by printing the bulletin board title on pieces of construction paper. Staple the title to the bulletin board.

4. Cut rectangular pieces of construction paper for the students' answers. Size them to fit the grid spaces while allowing the date to show.

5. Have each student select a date to research. When an event is found for that date, print the item on a rectangle and staple it in place on the calendar.

Game

Categories-Nobel Awards

OBJECTIVE The students will use an almanac to find the names of Nobel Award winners.

DESCRIPTION Teams or individuals compete to fill in the most names on a grid.

MATERIALS
- ditto master for game sheet
- pencil for each player or team
- almanac for each player or team

PROCEDURE
1. Prepare a ditto master of the categories game sheet.

NOBEL	A	W	A	R	D	S
Physics						
Chemistry						
Peace						
Literature						

2. Choose team or individual play and prepare the number of copies of the game sheet accordingly.
3. Explain the rules to the players:
   - a. The object of the game is to earn the most points by finding the most names to fill in the grid.
   - b. Use the almanac as your reference.
   - c. Each name must fit a category and must begin with a letter at the top of a column.
   - d. The time limit will be _____ .
   - e. When the time is up, one point is awarded for each correct name. The highest score wins.

Using the Fact Locator

Here is a portion of a typical almanac index.

Radio
actors, actresses 356
awards 357
inventions 765
stations, U.S. 931
Red Cross 154
Reno, Nevada 456–457
buildings 488
mayor 320
population 124,679
Rivers
dams 712–713

freight 592
United States 434
longest 687
world 688–689

Roosevelt, Franklin D. . . 264
birthday 837
Congress sessions 901
death 586
N.R.A. 918
wife, family 420
Ross, Betsy 259

A. Use the index above. Tell the page number on which you might find each of the facts below. (You may not be able to find them all.)

_____ 1. What is the world's longest river?

_____ 2. Did President Roosevelt have children?

_____ 3. Is Johnny Carson a radio actor?

_____ 4. What is the tallest building in Reno, Nevada?

_____ 5. How many major dams are there in California?

_____ 6. How much rye did Canada produce last year?

_____ 7. Which U.S. river has the most tributaries?

_____ 8. When was Betsy Ross born?

B. Use the index above to name the subtopic that would help you answer each question below.

_____ 1. How many tons of freight were shipped on the Mississippi River last year?

_____ 2. Is the Colorado River longer than the Missouri River?

_____ 3. Who invented the radio?

_____ 4. How many people live in Reno, Nevada?

Which Department?

A. The almanac will give you up-to-date information. Use it when you want the most recent facts. Read the list of research questions below. Write *yes* if the almanac would be the best reference book because you need up-to-date facts. If another type of reference book would be more helpful, name the type of book you would use.

_____yes_____ a. Who won the college basketball championship last year?

____encyclopedia____ b. Did George Washington write the Constitution of the United States?

_____ 1. Who is the governor of Texas?

_____ 2. How many square miles are there in the state of Ohio?

_____ 3. When will be the next eclipse of the sun?

_____ 4. When did William Penn begin the colony of Pennsylvania?

_____ 5. Who holds the record for the most hours of space travel?

_____ 6. What is the population of New York City?

_____ 7. How is steel made?

_____ 8. How much steel did Japan produce last year?

B. Now you are ready to find the "departments" in the big "store" of facts called the almanac. The key to this store is the index, which is usually found in the *front* of the almanac. There may also be a short index in the back. Use the index of an almanac to find the entry for your state. Name five subtopics listed for your state.

_____

_____

_____

I. M. A. Booksnoop reproducible page, copyright © 1983

Department. Please!

A. In a large department store like the almanac, you need to know which "section," or index topic, will help you find the fact you want. Write which topic you would look for in the index to help answer each question below.

_____football_____   a. How many touchdowns did O. J. Simpson score?

_____presidents_____   b. When did Thomas Jefferson serve as the President of the United States?

_____ 1. How many home runs did Hank Aaron hit?

_____ 2. How many weather satellites are still operating?

_____ 3. Who invented touch-tone dialing?

_____ 4. How many automobiles were sold in the United States last year?

_____ 5. Who is the president of the United Nations?

_____ 6. What products does the Republic of South Africa produce besides gold?

_____ 7. Which place in the United States had the coldest temperature last year?

_____ 8. Which country produced the most coffee last year?

_____ 9. What is the current automobile speed record and who holds it?

_____ 10. How many moons does Saturn have?

B. Use the almanac to find the answers to five of the questions listed above. Write the number of each question and the answer.

_____

_____

_____

_____

_____

Only the Facts, Please!

Detectives have to know how to ask questions. Use the index in your almanac to find the page numbers for each main entry listed below. Read the information about each entry and write an interesting question about it. Write the answer, too.

1. Animals: pages _____ to _____

Question: _____

Answer: _____

2. Inventions: pages _____ to _____

Question: _____

Answer: _____

3. Trees: pages _____ to _____

Question: _____

Answer: _____

4. Volcanoes: pages _____ to _____

Question: _____

Answer: _____

5. Weather—Record Temperatures: pages _____ to _____

Question: _____

Answer: _____

6. Tornadoes: pages _____ to _____

Question: _____

Answer: _____

Almanac Test

A. For each question below, write *yes* if the almanac would be the best reference book to use to answer the question. Write *no* if another reference book would be more helpful.

_____ 1. Who holds the record for the mile run?

_____ 2. How are laser rays controlled?

_____ 3. How did Alabama get its name?

_____ 4. What are some of Benjamin Franklin's famous sayings?

_____ 5. Is the Nile River longer than the Amazon River?

_____ 6. Who holds the record for the longest punt?

_____ 7. Did George Washington visit France while he was president?

_____ 8. Who wrote *A Midsummer Night's Dream*?

_____ 9. How many kings of England have been named Henry?

_____ 10. How many people live in Washington, D.C.?

B. Write which main topic you would look for to help you answer each question below.

_____ 1. What is the world's biggest animal?

_____ 2. How many barrels of oil did the United States import last year?

_____ 3. Did Abraham Lincoln have any brothers and sisters?

_____ 4. What is the largest lake in Minnesota?

_____ 5. Who holds the track record for the Indianapolis 500?

Unit 9

The Encyclopedia

Objective

The students will become familiar with the scope and limitations of an encyclopedia and will locate specific information in available encyclopedias.

Before You Begin

Alphabetizing and index skills allow easy access to the information in an encyclopedia. Use the activities in units 1 and 2 to refine your students' skills in these areas. Note taking rather than verbatim copying should be stressed as you present the second and fourth activities in this unit.

Motivational Riddle
Can You Find It?

SUGGESTIONS FOR USE   Use this riddle as the conclusion to your introduction of the encyclopedia. Attach the riddle to the magnifying glass in the Booksnoop poster. Have your students make pairs of rhyming questions to replace lines seven and eight of the riddle.

RIDDLE

For Garfield, glaciers, and gold, look in G.
Tolstoy and Texas you will find in T.
For facts about everything—from armadilloes to Morse—
Your encyclopedia is just the source.
Here are a few questions made to puzzle you.
Let's give it a try to see what you can do.
Who in the world made the first printing press?
What creature supposedly lives in Loch Ness?
When was the start of the French Revolution?
In your encyclopedia you'll find each solution.
   Answers: Johann Gutenberg; the Loch Ness monster; 1789

Bulletin Board
I'm in a Pickle!

OBJECTIVE   The students will use the encyclopedia to answer questions.

DESCRIPTION   The students get out of a "pickle" by finding the answers to teacher-prepared questions. The questions and answers are written on pickles.

MATERIALS

- green and brown construction paper
- black felt-tip pen
- scissors
- small box, at least six inches long
- stapler
- encyclopedia

PROCEDURE

1. Prepare a list of questions. You will need at least one question for each student. We found the almanac to be a great source of question ideas.

2. Make the caption. Cut out I'M IN A from construction paper. Cut out a large green pickle and print PICKLE on it. Staple these to the bulletin board.

3. Cut the pickle barrel from brown construction paper. Use a black felt-tip pen to highlight the barrel and label it Pickle Barrel. Staple the barrel in position on the bulletin board.

4. Cover the small box with brown construction paper. Staple one side of the box to the top of the pickle barrel. Label the box Pickle Questions.

5. Prepare the question and answer pickles on green construction paper. You will need a small pickle and a large pickle for each question. Make extra pickles if you want this bulletin board to be an on-going activity. Cut out the pickles and print a question on each small pickle. Put the question pickles in the pickle barrel box.

Where is the
Erie Canal located and
when was it built?

Name _Joe Smith_____
Encyclopedia_____Vol._____
Answer _____
_____
_____

6. Present the bulletin board to your students. Have each student choose a question pickle and answer the question. Give them large pickles on which to write their answers. Then staple each question pickle beside its answer pickle on the bulletin board. Soon the bulletin board will be covered with information gained from the encyclopedia.

7. When all of your questions have been answered, challenge your students to prepare their own question pickles.

Games
Verify the Facts

OBJECTIVE The students will use encyclopedias to verify statements.

DESCRIPTION Teams compete to be the first to verify a given list of facts. Finding entries quickly and skimming material are the skills enhanced by this game.

MATERIALS
- ditto masters
- sets of encyclopedias
- pencil and game sheet for each team

PROCEDURE
1. Before the day of the game, divide your students into teams of four or five players each. Assign a set of encyclopedias or a portion of a set to each team.

2. Prepare a list of statements, some true, some false, for each team to verify. (See the sample below.) Make the difficulty and number of statements commensurate with the abilities of your students. Each statement must be verifiable in the set (or portion of the set) of encyclopedias assigned to that team. For example, if team 1 is assigned volumes A–L, their game sheet statements must contain information found in volumes A–L.

3. Put the game sheets on ditto masters so that you can use this game with other groups.

4. On the day of the game, assign the students to their teams and encyclopedias.

5. Explain the rules:
   a. The object of the game is to score the most points.
   b. Each team will be given a list of statements that can be verified in the encyclopedias given to the team.
   c. Choose a recorder for your team.
   d. Read all the statements and decide if each is true or false. The recorder writes *true* or *false* to show the team opinion. These cannot be changed.
   e. The team consults the encyclopedias to find the facts that verify the statements. The recorder writes the facts as they are located.

f. The scoring is one point for each correct true or false, five points for each correct fact, and a bonus of one point for each correct fact to the team that finishes first.

6. Variation (teacher timesaver): Have the predetermined teams prepare the game sheets.

SAMPLE GAME SHEET ITEM

1. Statement: According to Greek mythology, Pegasus was a flying horse.

Team opinion: _____

Encyclopedia: Volume _____ Page _____

Fact: _____

_____

Encyclopedia Categories

OBJECTIVE The students will use the encyclopedia to locate entries that fit given categories.

PROCEDURE

1. See the almanac version of this game, page 80, for the basic setup. Then adjust it as follows.

2. Make teams of five players each.

3. Use volumes of the encyclopedia as the headings of the columns.

4. Use Country, Person, Element, Animal, and Invention as the categories.

5. Change rule c to: "Each item must fit a category, must begin with a letter at the top of a column, and must be an entry in your encyclopedia."

Finding the Keys

A. An encyclopedia detective needs keys—key words that is! What is the key word you would look under to find the answer to each question below?

_____ 1. What is the difference between an aneroid barometer and a mercury barometer?

_____ 2. Where was the civilization of the Incas located?

_____ 3. How is gasoline made?

_____ 4. When did the dodo become extinct?

_____ 5. How does a helicopter fly?

_____ 6. What training did a knight receive?

_____ 7. Where do plastics come from?

_____ 8. What is the speed of light?

_____ 9. How do you tie a bowline knot?

_____ 10. What is natural immunity?

B. Sometimes you will need to use cross-references and the encyclopedia's index. Match each key word below with a cross-reference.

Key Word	**Cross-reference**
____ 1. Comets	a. *see also* Textiles
____ 2. Nervous system	b. *see also* Solar system
____ 3. Robins	c. *see also* Human body
____ 4. Water cycle	d. *see also* Birds
____ 5. Linen	e. *see also* Weather

Using the Keys

A. Before you unlock your encyclopedia, check the copyright date. What does the copyright date tell you about the information in the

encyclopedia? _____

_____

B. Now you will have to use your set of encyclopedias. Write the

name of your set. _____
   Choose one of the following topics to research. Circle your choice.

albatrosses	jellyfish	submarines
bananas	kangaroos	tin
crocodiles	lions	unicorns
diamonds	mastodons	volcanoes
ermines	nickel	whales
flags	orangutans	xenon
grasshoppers	platypuses	yaks
heraldry	Quebec	zodiac
Iceland	radio	

C. Locate your topic in the encyclopedia and read the information. Look for five important facts. Write these facts in phrases below. (A good note-taker does not need to copy complete sentences.)

1. _____

2. _____

3. _____

4. _____

5. _____

D. Write your notes in paragraph form on another piece of paper.

Who Did It?

A. When you are looking for information about a person, you must use the last name to locate the entry. If a person is royalty and does not use a last name, you would look under the first name; for example, to find Queen Elizabeth II, you would look under *Elizabeth*. Write the letter of the volume you would use to locate each name below.

___ 1. Harry S. Truman   ___ 4. Amelia Earhart

___ 2. King George III   ___ 5. Eli Whitney

___ 3. Anton Dvorak   ___ 6. Lady Jane Grey

B. Now you are ready to use your encyclopedia to find out "who did it." Below is a list of inventions. Find out who invented each one. Write the volume and the page number where you found the answer, and write the name of the inventor. (There may be more than one name.)

Invention	Vol.	Page	Inventor(s)
1. Adding machine	___	___	_____
2. Air conditioning	___	___	_____
3. Electric battery	___	___	_____
4. Elevator	___	___	_____
5. Cash register	___	___	_____
6. Dynamite	___	___	_____
7. Gasoline engine	___	___	_____
8. Geiger counter	___	___	_____
9. Modern bicycle	___	___	_____
10. Kaleidoscope	___	___	_____
11. Motorcycle	___	___	_____
12. Oleomargarine	___	___	_____
13. Parachute	___	___	_____

NAME _____

Discover the Details

A detective must know a lot about the world. Read the projects below. Each can be researched in an encyclopedia. Choose a project to research. (This is the hardest part. Choose carefully and stick to your choice.)

1. How are coded messages cracked? Make some coded messages using famous codes. Prepare them in chart form.

2. How did our system for telling time develop? Take notes and then prepare an oral or written report. Show the world time zones on a map.

3. Was our calendar always the way it is now? List the changes that have taken place. Make a chart showing how the months got their names.

4. The world of stars is endless. Find out how stars are classified by scientists and write the information in chart form. Make diagrams of at least five constellations.

5. Find out about rocks. Learn the names of the rocks found in your area. Make a rock collection and label your findings.

6. Find out about trees. Learn the names of the trees found in your area. Make a leaf collection and label each leaf. Draw a cross section of a typical tree trunk. Label the parts.

7. How many bones are in the human body? Make a diagram of the human skeleton and label the largest bones. Write a report explaining different types of bone fractures.

8. How are weather predictions made? Prepare an oral or written report about instruments that meteorologists use to predict weather. Include diagrams.

9. Where did our number system originate? Make charts of other number systems. Write a paragraph summarizing the history of our decimal system.

10. Did you ever wonder how a ship knows where it is going in the middle of the ocean? Prepare an oral or written report about navigation. Try to find a navigator's chart to include with your report.

Discover the Details *continued*

11. What is a laser? How does it work? How are they useful to us? Prepare an oral or written report to answer these questions. Include diagrams.

12. How have clothing styles changed in the last 200 years? List the periods of clothing styles. Illustrate your information.

13. Oil is an important natural resource. How was oil formed? How is oil changed into gasoline? Prepare an oral or written report. Include diagrams.

14. Choose a president of the United States who is not well known. Write a biographical sketch about him.

15. Write a biographical sketch about one of these famous women: Elizabeth C. Stanton, Marie Curie, Florence Nightingale, Harriet Tubman, Maria Mitchell, Harriet Beecher Stowe, Susan B. Anthony, or Elizabeth I.

16. How does a gasoline engine work? Prepare a diagram of an engine. Write an explanation of each main part. Explain the difference between diesel engines and gasoline engines.

17. Research the history of flight. Make a time line of the main events. Be sure to include enough information to make your time line informative. Add illustrations for more interest.

18. Investigate the history of your favorite sport. Prepare an oral or written report. Include diagrams if possible.

19. Research the steps in preparing a typical television show from script development to broadcast. Present your information in a flowchart if you know how, or present your facts in a cartoon or a written report.

20. Choose your own topic for research. List the things you wish to find out and have your teacher approve it first.

Encyclopedia Test

A. Read each statement. Then write *true* or *false* in the blank.

_____ 1. An encyclopedia never has an index.

_____ 2. You should check the copyright date of an encyclopedia before you use the information.

_____ 3. Entries in an encyclopedia are arranged by age, from oldest to newest.

_____ 4. There may be more than one place in the encyclopedia that has information about your topic.

_____ 5. People are listed by their last names in an encyclopedia.

B. Circle the key word or words in each question below that would help you find the encyclopedia entry to answer the question. Then write the letter of the volume you would use in the blank.

____ 1. What are the phases of the moon?

____ 2. What is the number of known elements?

____ 3. How is the length of a calendar year determined?

____ 4. Who introduced the use of antiseptics?

____ 5. Which explorer discovered Alaska?

____ 6. How do plants take in water and food?

____ 7. When was the French and Indian War?

____ 8. What causes an eclipse?

____ 9. Why was Marco Polo important?

____ 10. Why do we remember King Henry VIII?

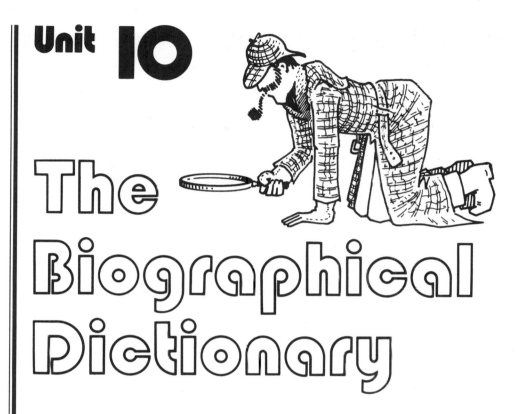

Unit 10

The Biographical Dictionary

Objective

The students will become familiar with the contents, use, and limitations of a biographical dictionary.

Before You Begin

All of the activities in this unit require the use of *Webster's Biographical Dictionary*. Since most schools usually have a limited number of copies of this book, we suggest you use the worksheets as learning centers. To be sure all students are exposed to the biographical dictionary, use the bulletin board, World's Most Wanted Wonderful Winners, pages 98–99. Obtain copies of the other types of biographical dictionaries and make them available to your group, too.

Motivational Riddle
He Spread Light

SUGGESTIONS FOR USE   Use this riddle to introduce your students to the biographical dictionary as a time saver. Attach the riddle to the magnifying glass in the Booksnoop poster. When a few basic facts about a person are required, a biographical dictionary is the reference of preference!

RIDDLE

In my last, my first is <u>E</u>.
My second is the fourth, you'll see.
Through my third, my fourth—a snake—is seen.
My fifth is round and not very lean.
My sixth is in <u>not</u> but not in <u>dot</u>.
Look me over, what have you got?
An American man, you might say,
Who spread his light in a special way!
   Answer: Thomas A. Edison

Bulletin Board
World's Most Wanted Wonderful Winners

OBJECTIVE   The students will use the biographical dictionary to match famous people with their descriptions.

DESCRIPTION   Stars and pictures of famous people highlight this bulletin board. Short biographies are written on cards, and the students use the biographical dictionary to make matches.

SUGGESTIONS FOR USE   Use this bulletin board to introduce the biographical dictionary to your group. Then have your students find pictures of famous people and write the matching biographies.

MATERIALS
- biographical dictionary
- yellow construction paper
- scissors
- tagboard
- pushpins
- hole punch
- pictures of famous people

PROCEDURE

1. Choose pictures of people who are listed in the biographical dictionary. The number you choose will depend on the area of your bulletin board.

2. Cut out a star from yellow construction paper for each picture. Staple the stars to the bulletin board.

3. Mount each picture on tagboard. Number the tagboard and write the person's name on it. Fasten each picture on or beside a star. Place a pushpin at the bottom of each picture.

4. Prepare the biography cards. Cut squares of tagboard that go well with the size of your stars. Punch a hole in each card about 1 inch from the top.

5. Write a biographical facts card for each picture. Include a few nonmatches if you wish. Assign a letter to each card.

6. Place several pushpins near the bottom of the bulletin board and hang the facts cards on them.

7. Prepare the caption and staple it to the bulletin board.

8. Write the challenge rhyme on a piece of construction paper and staple it to the bulletin board. The rhyme is:

> What did these talented persons do?
> The biographical dictionary will give you a clue.
> Look up the facts, and pick the right card.
> Hang it under the picture—that's not hard!
> Check your answers and put the cards back when you're through.

9. Make an answer key, cover it with a flap, and staple it to the bulletin board.

Game
Unscramble

OBJECTIVE The students will unscramble a set of letters to find a famous person's last name and use the biographical dictionary to find the first name.

DESCRIPTION A teacher-prepared game sheet challenges the students to discover the hidden names. Biographical clues are given. Then the biographical dictionary is checked to find the first names.

SUGGESTIONS FOR USE This game lends itself to team or individual play. Make it an individual activity if your supply of biographical dictionaries is limited. The frustration level may be too high for less able students.

MATERIALS
- game sheet and pencil for each player or team
- biographical dictionary for each player or team

PROCEDURE

1. Decide if you wish to make Unscramble a team game or an individual activity. Reproduce the appropriate number of game sheets. You will need a sheet for each individual or a sheet for each team.

2. For team play, explain the rules:
   a. The object of the game is to be the first team to unscramble all the famous persons' last names and find their first names in the biographical dictionary.
   b. Each team will be given a dictionary, a game sheet, and a pencil. When the signal is given, begin unscrambling.
   c. When all teams are finished, the team with the most correct answers is the winner.

SAMPLE GAMESHEET: UNSCRAMBLE

Directions: Unscramble the last names in column 2. Use the biographical dictionary to find the first names and write them in column 3. The clues in column 4 will help you. Write the first letter of each last name in column 1. The correct letters will spell the last name of another famous person.

1	2	3	4
___	staeanm	_____ , _____	Kodak camera man
___	nivgir	_____ , _____	Author
___	dansgrbu	_____ , _____	Poet
___	rahtare	_____ , _____	Aviator
___	sant	_____ , _____	Cartoonist
___	yeash	_____ , _____	U.S. president
___	soit	_____ , _____	Elevator man
___	swihlert	_____ , _____	Artist
___	stnieien	_____ , _____	Physicist
___	veerer	_____ , _____	American patriot

ANSWERS: Eastman, George; **I**rving, Washington; **S**andburg, Carl; **E**arhart, Amelia; **N**ast, Thomas; **H**ayes, Rutherford B.; **O**tis, Elisha; **W**histler, James A. M.; **E**instein, Albert; **R**evere, Paul

Biographical Dictionary Page

Jeffers	777	Jelačić od Bužima

Jef'fers (jĕf'ẽrz), **Robinson,** *in full* **John Robinson.** 1887–1962. American poet, b. Pittsburgh, Pa. Author of *Californians* (1916), *Tamar* (1924), *Cawdor* (1928), *Dear Judas* (1929), *Thurso's Landing* (1932), *Solstice* (1935), *Such Counsels You Gave to Me* (1937), etc.

Jeffers, William Martin. 1876–1953. American railway official, b. North Platte, Nebr.; rose from office boy (1890) to president (1937–46) of Union Pacific R.R.; U.S. rubber administrator (1942–43).

Jef'fer·son (jĕf'ẽr·s'n), **Charles Edward.** 1860–1937. American Congregational clergyman; pastor of Broadway Tabernacle, New York City (1898–1937).

Jefferson, Joseph. 1829–1905. American actor, b. Philadelphia; made success in Laura Keene's company, New York, as Asa Trenchard in *Our American Cousin* (1858), and Caleb Plummer in *The Cricket on the Hearth* (1859). Most famous role, Rip Van Winkle in Dion Boucicault's play of that name (from 1865). Also made success of Bob Acres in *The Rivals* (from 1880). His grandfather **Joseph Jefferson** (1774–1832), b. Plymouth, Eng., came to U.S. (1795) and appeared chiefly in comedy roles. See also Eleanor FARJEON.

Jefferson, Thomas. 1743–1826. Third president of the United States, b. in Goochland, now Albemarle County, Va. Grad. William and Mary (1762). Adm. to bar (1767). Member, Virginia House of Burgesses (1769–74); with R. H. Lee and Patrick Henry initiated intercolonial committee of correspondence (1773). Member, Continental Congress (1775, 1776); chairman of committee that prepared Declaration of Independence; wrote and presented first draft of declaration to Congress (July 2, 1776); signed Declaration of Independence. Governor of Virginia (1779–81). Again member, Continental Congress (1783–85). U.S. minister to France (1785–89). U.S. secretary of state (1790–93); differing policies caused bitter antagonism with Alexander Hamilton, secretary of treasury. Vice-president of the U.S. (1797–1801); president of the U.S. (1801–09), elected by House of Representatives after tie in popular vote (with Aaron Burr, *q.v.*). Features of administration: purchase of Louisiana, war against Algerian pirates, westward expansion, diplomatic trouble with Great Britain over impressment of American seamen (Embargo Act of 1807), prohibition of the importation of slaves. On retirement from presidency, lived on plantation at "Monticello," near Charlottesville, Va. Instrumental in founding U. of Virginia (1819). Elected to American Hall of Fame (1900).

Jef'frey (jĕf'rĭ), **Francis. Lord Jeffrey.** 1773–1850. Scottish critic and jurist, b. in Edinburgh. One of founders of *Edinburgh Review* (1802), and its editor (1803–29). Judge of Court of Session (1834–50). Author of the famous devastating criticism of Wordsworth's *Excursion* beginning "This will never do."

Jef'freys (jĕf'rĭz), **George. 1st Baron Jeffreys of Wem** (wĕm). 1644–1689. English jurist. Solicitor general to duke of York (1677). Lord chief justice (1682) and privy councilor (1683); lord chancellor (1685). On overthrow of James II, attempted to flee from England but was captured and imprisoned in Tower of London (1688), where he died (April 18, 1689). As chief justice and chancellor, made himself notorious by injustice and brutality. The assizes conducted by him (1685) at which those involved in Monmouth's rebellion against James II were tried became known as the Bloody Assizes because of the number of executions decreed.

Jef'fries (jĕf'rĭz), **James J.** 1875–1953. American prizefighter; world heavyweight champion from 1899 (winning title from Bob Fitzsimmons) until he retired in 1905; returned to ring for match with Jack Johnson (1910), in which he was defeated.

Jeffries, John. 1744–1819. Physician and balloonist, b. Boston; practiced medicine in Boston. Loyalist during American Revolution; resident in England after the war. Interested himself in use of balloons for scientific observations and experiments; with François Blanchard, French aeronaut, crossed English Channel from Dover to forest of Guînes, France, in balloon (Jan. 7, 1785), first crossing of English Channel by air.

Jehan. See SHAH JAHAN.

Jehangir. See JAHANGIR.

Je·ho'a·haz (jĕ·hō'ā·hăz). See AHAZ.

Jehoahaz. *In Douay Bible* **Jo'a·chaz** (jō'ā·kăz). (1) King of Israel (d. 800? B.C.); son and successor of Jehu; reigned (c. 816–800 B.C.); his kingdom at mercy of Damascus (*2 Kings* xiii). (2) *Called* **Shal'lum** (shăl'ŭm) in *Jeremiah* xxii. 11. King of Judah; son of Josiah; reigned few months only (608 or 607 B.C.); deposed by Necho (II); carried as prisoner to Egypt, where he died (*2 Kings* xxiii. 30–33).

Jehoash. See JOASH.

Je·hoi'a·chin (jĕ·hoi'ā·kĭn). *In Douay Bible* **Jo'a·chin** (jō'ā·kĭn). 615?–?560 B.C. King of Judah (598 or 597 B.C.); son of Jehoiakim; reigned few months only; with Judean leaders, carried away as prisoner to Babylon by Nebuchadnezzar; held captive 37 years; released by Evil-Merodach (*2 Kings* xxiv. 6–16).

Je·hoi'a·kim (jĕ·hoi'ā·kĭm). *In Douay Bible* **Jo'a·kim** (jō'ā·kĭm). d. 598? B.C. King of Judah (c. 608–598 B.C.). Son of Josiah. Placed on throne by Necho (II), who had deposed Jehoahaz (*2 Kings* xxiii. 34–xxiv. 7); revolted against Babylon after hegemony over Palestine passed (605) from Necho to Nebuchadnezzar at battle of Carchemish; died at siege of Jerusalem just before city was taken; succeeded by Jehoiachin (*q.v.*).

Je·ho'ram (jĕ·hō'răm). *In Douay Bible* **Jo'ram** (jō'răm). (1) King of Israel (d. 843? B.C.); son of Ahab; succeeded older brother Ahaziah as king (c. 852–843 B.C.); with Jehoshaphat of Judah, put down revolt in Moab (*2 Kings* iii); revolt against him by Elisha and his party; slain by Jehu, who seized throne (*2 Kings* ix). (2) King of Judah (d. 844? B.C.); son and successor of Jehoshaphat; reigned (c. 851–844 B.C.); m. Athaliah (*q.v.*), daughter of Ahab and Jezebel; during his reign Edom rebelled; succeeded by son Ahaziah (*2 Kings* viii. 16–29; *2 Chron.* xxi).

Je·hosh'a·phat (jĕ·hŏsh'ā·făt). *In Douay Bible* **Jos'a·phat** (jŏs'ā·făt). d. 851? B.C. Son and successor of Asa. King of Judah (c. 875–851 B.C.). Ruled righteously and introduced reforms; made alliance with Israel and joined Ahab in battle at Ramoth Gilead against Syrians; practically vassal of Israel; succeeded by son Jehoram (*1 Kings* xxii. 41–50; *2 Kings* iii; *2 Chron.* xvii–xxi).

Je·hosh'e·ba (jĕ·hŏsh'ē·bà). *In Douay Bible* **Jos'a·ba** (jŏs'ā·bà). fl. 9th century B.C. Daughter of King Jehoram of Judah and aunt of Joash. With her husband, high priest Jehoiada, saved life of Joash when royal family was massacred by Athaliah (*2 Kings* xi. 2–3).

Je'hu (jē'hū). d. 816? B.C. King of Israel (c. 843–816 B.C.). Founder of new dynasty; soldier under King Ahab; led revolt against him; anointed king by Elisha; killed kings Jehoram and Ahaziah, driving his chariot furiously (*2 Kings* ix. 20) to the attack; seized throne of Israel and controlled Judah by destroying royal family; paid tribute to Shalmaneser III; at war with Hazael of Damascus; succeeded by son Jehoahaz (*2 Kings* ix–x).

Jehudah *or* **Jehuda.** Var. of JUDAH.

Je'la·čić od Bu'ži·ma (yĕ'lä·chĕt'y' [*Angl.* -chĭch] ŏd bōō'zhĕ·mä), Count **Josip.** 1801–1859. Croatian general and governor; lieutenant field marshal and ban of

chair; ḡo; sing; then, thin; verdure (16), nature (54); ĸ=ch in Ger. ich, ach; Fr. boɴ; yet; zh=z in azure. For explanation of abbreviations, etc., see the page immediately preceding the main vocabulary.

Who Am I?

The biographical dictionary is the best place to find out basic facts about famous people. Because this reference book tries to include every famous person, the amount of information given for each person is limited. The more well known people usually have larger entries.

A. Find out why we remember the people listed below. Write what each person did and the dates he or she lived.

Person	Dates	Accomplishment
1. George Washington Carver	_____	_____
2. Grandma Moses	_____	_____
3. John B. Dunlop	_____	_____
4. Harry M. Warner	_____	_____
5. George Westinghouse	_____	_____
6. Alexander Fleming	_____	_____
7. William Herschel	_____	_____
8. Lise Meitner	_____	_____
9. Marie Curie	_____	_____
10. Luther Burbank	_____	_____

B. Name a book written by each author listed below. If more than one title is listed, write the first one.

1. Rachel Carson _____

2. Edgar Rice Burroughs _____

3. Pearl Buck _____

4. Paul Zindel _____

5. Gwendolyn Brooks _____

Aliases

Many famous people are better known by their pseudonyms (pen names), nicknames, or professional names. Each person below had another name. Find the entry for each person and write his or her other name. Also tell what each person was or did.

Name	Other Name	Career
1. George H. Ruth	_____	_____
2. Samuel Clemens	_____	_____
3. Jonathan Swift	_____	_____
4. Harry Houdini	_____	_____
5. Kyriakos Theotokopoulos	_____	_____
6. Mohandas Karamchand Gandhi	_____	_____
7. William F. Cody	_____	_____
8. Henry Lee	_____	_____
9. Florence Nightingale	_____	_____
10. William H. Bonney	_____	_____
11. William Jennings Bryan	_____	_____
12. Mary Ann Evans	_____	_____
13. John XXIII	_____	_____
14. Anthony Wayne	_____	_____
15. Joan of Arc (Jeanne d'Arc)	_____	_____

How are We Related?

Below are some famous names listed in groups of three. Find the entries for the names in the biographical dictionary. Tell how the names in each set are related.

Example:

George Washington
Abraham Lincoln
Woodrow Wilson

_____U.S. presidents_____

Names	**Relationship**
1. George Catlin Georgia O'Keefe Winslow Homer	_____
2. Christopher Carson Daniel Boone Sacajawea	_____
3. Warren de la Rue Eli Whitney Johann C. Denner	_____
4. James K. Polk William H. Harrison James A. Garfield	_____
5. Cole Porter George Gershwin Irving Berlin	_____
6. George McClellan George Patton William T. Sherman	_____
7. Mary Lyon Emma Willard Maria Montessori	_____
8. Mary Baker Eddy Joseph Smith John Wesley	_____

Biographical Dictionary Test

A. Read each statement below. Write *true* or *false* next to each one.

_____ 1. The biographical dictionary lists names alphabetically.

_____ 2. A famous person may have more than one name.

_____ 3. The information always tells you if the person married and how many children he or she had.

_____ 4. The biographical dictionary lists all the books a famous author may have written.

_____ 5. A biographical dictionary contains all the facts you need for a report about a famous person.

_____ 6. The biographical dictionary will tell you if there are other ways to spell a person's name.

_____ 7. Names that begin with *Mc* are listed as though they begin with *Mac*.

_____ 8. Everything a famous person did is listed in the person's entry.

B. Use the biographical dictionary to find the names of famous inventors, authors, and political leaders. Write three names for each.

Inventors	Authors	Political Leaders
_____	_____	_____
_____	_____	_____
_____	_____	_____

Unit 11

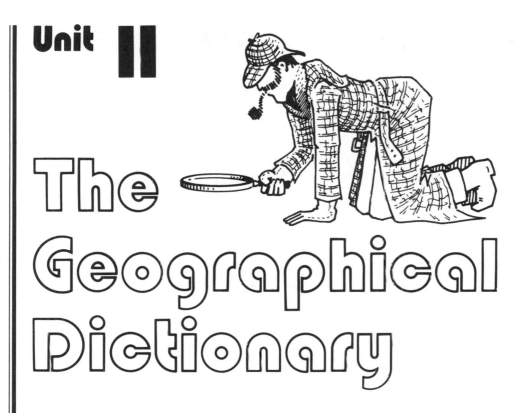

The Geographical Dictionary

Objective

The students will become familiar with the scope and limitations of a geographical dictionary.

Before You Begin

Map-reading skills are not a prerequisite for this unit. The activities direct your students to browse through the geographical dictionary looking for specific items. As in most reference book use, knowledge of the alphabet and the ability to use guide words are needed.

Motivational Riddle
A Popular Name Game

SUGGESTIONS FOR USE Use this riddle at the end of your introductory lesson about the geographical dictionary. If you are presenting the riddle to a small group, use a ditto. If you are presenting the riddle to your group as a whole, attach the riddle to the magnifying glass in the Booksnoop poster. If you plan to use this unit as enrichment, use the riddle as a challenge; then have the students find their own popular names and give the clues in riddle form.

RIDDLE

You'll find me in Arkansas, Australia, Maine, and Wales,
In Washington, twice in England, and, if all else fails,
In Vermont, New Hampshire, Oregon, and Tennessee.
Look in Minnesota, Rhode Island, and Kentucky.
My first syllable can mean the opposite of old.
My second means where ships could dock, I'm told.
  Answer: Newport

Bulletin Board
Where Is It?

OBJECTIVE The students will use a geographical dictionary to determine the correct locations of cities and nations.

DESCRIPTION The outlines of continents highlight this bulletin board. Your students are asked to match nations or cities with their continents.

MATERIALS

- scissors
- stapler
- tagboard
- pushpins
- hole punch
- overhead projector
- transparency
- pen
- paper
- world map

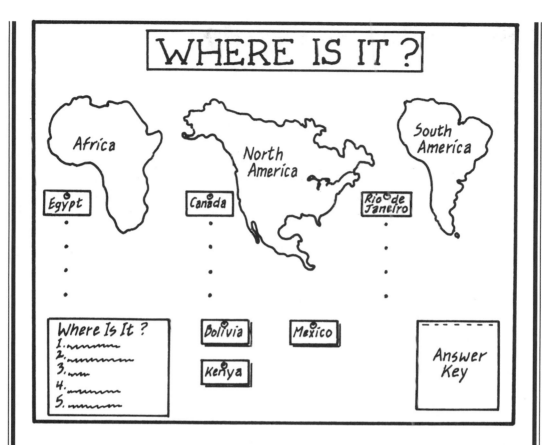

PROCEDURE

1. Choose three continents. Use the overhead projector to enlarge them for your bulletin board. Trace them onto backing paper or other paper and cut them out. Staple the continents to your bulletin board.

2. Make a list of cities and nations that are on the continents you have chosen.

3. Cut a 3-by-7 inch rectangle from tagboard for each city and nation. Print a name of a city or nation on each card. Punch a hole in each card about 1 inch from the top.

4. Place several pushpins near the bottom of the bulletin board and hang the cards on them.

5. Prepare the caption and staple it in position on the bulletin board.

6. Prepare an answer key by printing the answers on a piece of paper and covering them with a flap. Staple the answer key to the bulletin board.

7. Place a geographical dictionary at the bulletin board.

8. Print the following directions on a piece of paper and staple it to the bulletin board.

Where Is It?

1. Read the name cards.
2. Use the geographical dictionary to find the continent to which each nation or city belongs.
3. Hang each card under the correct continent.
4. Check your answers with the answer key.
5. Return the name cards to the storage pins when finished.

The Geographical Dictionary 109

Game

From Last to First

OBJECTIVE The students will use a geographical dictionary to complete the game task.

DESCRIPTION The last letter of a city is the first letter of the next city the contestants must find in the geographical dictionary. Browsing through this reference with a goal will widen your students' horizons.

SUGGESTIONS FOR USE Use this game at any time during the unit. The minimal teacher preparation needed gives this game an added plus.

MATERIALS
- piece of paper and pencil for each team
- geographical dictionary for each team

PROCEDURE

1. Divide your group into the smallest teams possible. You will need a geographical dictionary for each team.

2. Explain the rules:

    a. The team that makes the longest list of city names within the time limit is the winner.

    b. The first player makes a City column and a Continent column on the team's game sheet.

    c. You will be given a starting city name. The first player uses the geographical dictionary to find a city whose name begins with the last letter of the starting city's name. The name of the city and its continent is written on the game sheet. The game sheet and geographical dictionary is passed to the second player.

    d. The second player finds and writes the name of a city that begins with the last letter of the city the first player wrote down and passes the game materials to the next player, and so on. The last player gives the materials to the first player.

    e. Continue to find and write the city and continent names until the time limit expires. The time limit is _____ minutes.

SAMPLE GAME SHEET

Starting city: Lima

City	Continent
Algiers	Africa
Seattle	North America
Edinburgh	Europe

Geographical Dictionary Page

Mary Esther   734   **Mascara**

Mary Es·ther \ˌmer-ē-'es-tər, ˌmar-ē-\. Town, Okaloosa co., NW Florida, 27 m. E of Pensacola; pop. (1970c) 3192.

Mary Island. See CANTON ISLAND.

Mar·y·land \'mer-ə-lənd\. 1 A middle Atlantic state of U.S.A., bounded on N by Pennsylvania, on E by Delaware and the Atlantic Ocean, on S by Virginia and West Virginia, and on W by West Virginia; 42d state in area, 10,577 sq. m. (land area 9881 sq. m.); 18th state in population, (1970c) 3,922,399; ✱ Annapolis; one of the original states of the Union, the 7th to ratify the Federal Constitution (Apr. 28, 1788).

Nicknames: Old Line State; Cockade State. *State flower:* Black-eyed Susan. *Motto:* Fatti Maschii, Parole Femine (Manly Deeds, Feminine Words). *Rivers:* Potomac, forming S boundary; Patuxent, flowing SE into Chesapeake Bay; Susquehanna, flowing across NE corner into headwaters of Chesapeake Bay. *Highest point:* Backbone Mt., 3360 ft., in Garrett co. *Chief products:* Dairy products, tobacco; livestock; fishing; manufacturing: primary metals, transportation equipment, chemicals, apparel. *Chief cities:* Baltimore, Rockville, Hagerstown, Bowie, Cumberland. See *Table of States* at UNITED STATES. Divided into the following 23 counties (for pronunciation of their names, see their individual entries):

NAME	LOCATION	AREA[1] (sq. m.)	POP. (1970c)	CO. SEAT
Allegany	NW	428	84,044	Cumberland
Anne Arundel	cen.	423	297,539	Annapolis
Baltimore	N	598[2]	621,871	Towson
Baltimore city[3]		75	905,759	
Calvert	S	217	20,682	Prince Frederick
Caroline	E	321	19,781	Denton
Carroll	N	456	69,006	Westminster
Cecil	NE corner	362	53,291	Elkton
Charles	S	459	47,678	La Plata
Dorchester	SE	594	29,405	Cambridge
Frederick	N	665	84,927	Frederick
Garrett	NW corner	659	21,476	Oakland
Harford	NE	453	115,378	Bel Air
Howard	cen.	251	62,394	Ellicott City
Kent	NE	281	16,146	Chestertown
Montgomery	cen.	496	522,809	Rockville
Prince Georges	S cen.	484	661,192	Upper Marlboro
Queen Annes	E	375	18,422	Centreville
Saint Marys	S	373	47,388	Leonardtown
Somerset	SE	339	18,924	Princess Anne
Talbot	E	261	23,682	Easton
Washington	N	459	103,829	Hagerstown
Wicomico	SE	381	54,236	Salisbury
Worcester	SE; coastal	479	24,442	Snow Hill

[1]Area = land area.
[2]Exclusive of city of Baltimore which is administratively independent of the county.
[3]Administratively independent of Baltimore co. and has itself the status of a county.

History: Granted to George Calvert (Lord Baltimore) as proprietary colony 1632; first American colony to achieve religious freedom; first settled at St. Marys 1634, which was its capital 1634–94; a royal colony 1689–1715; its boundary with Pennsylvania, in dispute from 1681, settled by drawing of Mason and Dixon's Line 1763–69; first constitutional convention Aug. 14–Nov. 11, 1776; adopted Articles of Confederation 1781; ceded territory for District of Columbia (*q.v.*); invaded by Confederate forces 1862; abolished slavery 1864; adopted present constitution 1867. See BALTIMORE.

2 The southernmost county of Liberia, W Africa; 1675 sq. m.; pop. (1967e) 67,809; set up as an independent African state 1833 by Negroes from the United States; annexed to Liberia 1857.

Mar·y·port \'me(ə)r-ē-ˌpō(ə)rt, 'ma(ə)r-ē-, -ˌpȯ(ə)rt\. Urban district, Cumberland, NW England, on Solway Firth at mouth of the Ellen, 28 m. SW of Carlisle; pop. (1971p) 11,615.

Mar·ys·vale Peak \ˌme(ə)r-ēz-ˌvāl-, ˌma(ə)r-ēz-\. Mountain, Piute co., S cen. Utah; 10,943 ft.

Mar·ys·ville \'me(ə)r-ēz-vil, 'ma(ə)r-ēz-\. 1 City, ⊗ of Yuba co., N cen. California, 42 m. N of Sacramento; pop. (1970c) 9353; fruit canning; fruit, dairy, and livestock farms; Yuba Coll. (1927).

2 City, ⊗ of Marshall co., NE Kansas, 45 m. N of Manhattan on Big Blue river; pop. (1970c) 3588; radar equipment; poultry-packing plant; diversified agriculture.

3 City, St. Clair co., SE Michigan, on St. Clair river 5 m. S of Port Huron; pop. (1970c) 5610.

4 Village, ⊗ of Union co., Ohio, 27 m. NW of Columbus; pop. (1970c) 5744; brass goods, plastics, lumber; dairy and grain farms.

5 Borough, Perry co., S cen. Pennsylvania, on Susquehanna river 8 m. N of Harrisburg; pop. (1970c) 2328.

6 Town, Snohomish co., NW cen. Washington, on Puget Sound 5 m. N of Everett; pop. (1970c) 4343; boats, shingles, leather goods; dairy farms.

7 Town, York co., SW New Brunswick, Canada, 5 m. N of Fredericton; pop. (1966c) 3572.

Maryūt, Buḥrayat. See MAREOTIS, LAKE.

Mar·y·ville \'mar-i-vəl, 'mer-, -ˌvil\. 1 City, ⊗ of Nodaway co., NW Missouri, 42 m. N of St. Joseph; pop. (1970c) 9970; tools, cement blocks; diversified agriculture; Northwest Missouri State Coll. (1905).

2 City, ⊗ of Blount co., E Tennessee, near Great Smoky Mts. National Park 15 m. S of Knoxville; pop. (1970c) 13,808; lumber, electronic components, fabricated aluminum; limestone quarries; tobacco, corn; Maryville Coll. (1819).

Ma·sa·da \mə-'säd-ə, -'sȧd-\. Fortified hill on W shore of Dead Sea at S end, SE Israel; fortifications constructed 1st cent. B.C.; in 72–73 A.D. scene of final stand of Jews against Romans (defenders killed themselves rather than surrender).

Más Afue·ra \ˌmäs-ə-'fwer-ə\ *or* Ale·jan·dro Sel·kirk \ˌäl-i-kän-drō-'sel-kirk\. An island of the Juan Fernández group. See JUAN FERNÁNDEZ.

Ma·san \'mäs-ˌän\ *or formerly* Ma·sam·po \mə-'säm-(ˌ)pō\. Seaport city, South Kyŏngsang prov., South Korea, at head of an inlet of Western Channel 26 m. W of Pusan; pop. (1970e) 190,992; a commercial and industrial center; opened to foreign trade 1899.

Masandam, Ras. See MUSANDAM, CAPE.

Masanutten Mountain. See MASSANUTTEN MOUNTAIN

Más a Tier·ra \ˌmäs-ə-tē-'er-ə\ *or* Ro·bin·son Cru·soe Island \ˌräb-ən-sən-'krü-ˌsō-\. An island of the Juan Fernández group. See JUAN FERNÁNDEZ.

Ma·sa·ya \mə-'sä-yə, -'sī-ə\. 1 Department of SW Nicaragua. See table at NICARAGUA.

2 Town, its ✱; pop. (1970e) 49,691; 5th largest city in Nicaragua; center of rich agricultural region; produces cigars, soap, leather goods, footwear, hats.

Mas·ba·te \mäs-'bät-ē\. 1 Island and province in Visayan Is., cen. Phil., S of SE Luzon; 1563 sq. m.; pop. (1970p) 492,868; ✱ Masbate. Formerly a subprovince of Sorsogon from which it is separated by Ticao Pass and Ticao I.; on the E borders on Samar Sea, on the S on Visayan Sea, and on the W on Sibuyan Sea; separated from NE Panay by Jintotolo Channel. Covered with mountains ranging from 1200 to 2000 ft. As province includes Burias I. and Ticao I. Produces sugarcane, cotton, hemp, and some rice; noted for its cattle and horses. Chief towns Masbate, Cataingan, Aroroy, Milagros, Dimasalang.

History: Explored by Spaniards in latter half of 16th cent.; long a part of Albay prov.; made separate comandancia 1846; under Americans received civil government Mar. 1901 and made subprovince of Sorsogon; created a province 1939; invaded by Americans Apr. 1945.

2 Municipality, ✱ of Masbate prov., Phil., on NE coast of Masbate I. opp. Ticao I.; pop. (1969e) 43,700; port of entry.

Mas·ca·ra \'mas-kə-rə\. Commune, SW Mostaganem dept., NW Algeria, 60 m. SE of Oran; pop. (1966c) 43,000; built on a mountain slope at alt. 1800 ft.; exports red and white wine, olive oil, grain. Importance increased when it became headquarters of Abd-el-Kader 1832; captured twice by French, 1835 and 1841, and considerably damaged.

By permission. From Webster's New Geographical Dictionary © 1980 by G. & C. Merriam Co., publishers of the Merriam-Webster Dictionaries.

Finding Your Way

Let's go traveling. The geographical dictionary can tell you about any place you'd like to go. Use your geographical dictionary to answer each question below.

_____ 1. On which page is the list of maps?

_____ 2. On which page do you find the map symbols?

_____ 3. What does the map symbol look like?

_____ 4. On which page do you find the list of abbreviations used in the book?

_____ 5. What is the first entry in the dictionary?

_____ 6. What is the last entry?

_____ 7. What place has your name or the name of a classmate?

_____ 8. How many entries begin with *Little*?

_____ 9. How many entries begin with *Big*?

_____ 10. Which is the more popular name for places—Lincoln or Washington?

_____ 11. Which color is the most popular for place names—blue, green, or red?

_____ 12. Is the place where you live listed?

_____ 13. What is another name for the Union of Soviet Socialist Republics?

_____ 14. Find the entry for Ottawa. Of what country is Ottawa the capital city?

I. M. A. Booksnoop reproducible page, copyright © 1983

Clues from First to Last

Be a geographical detective! Use the geographical dictionary to solve the clues below.

_____ 1. Find the island whose name begins with *gree* and ends with *d*. It is the world's largest island.

_____ 2. Find the lake that has the largest area of any lake in the world. Its name begins with *casp*. The second word of its name ends with an *a*.

_____ 3. The name of the world's longest river begins with *ni*. What is the name? How long _____ is this river?

_____ 4. The lowest point on earth has a two-word name. The first three letters of its name are *dea*, and the last letter is *a*. What is the name?

_____ 5. A famous volcano in Italy destroyed the ancient cities of Pompeii and Herculaneum. The volcano's name begins with *ves*. What is the full name?

_____ 6. The first two letters of the name of the world's largest desert are *sa*. What is this desert's name?

_____ 7. The world's largest waterfall has a two-word name. The first three letters are *ang*. What is its name?

_____ 8. This Pacific island is famous for its gigantic statues. The first two letters of its first name are *ea*. The last letter of its first name is *r*. What is its name?

_____ 9. This peak in South Dakota is known for its carved faces of four presidents. The first three letters of its second name are *rus*. What is its name?

Get the Geographical Facts

Dig a little deeper into the geographical dictionary to find the information requested below. If the question is not answered in your geographical dictionary, write *N.A.,* meaning "not available."

A. Find and read the entry for the <u>Amazon River</u>.

1. List five facts about this river.

   a. _____

   b. _____

   c. _____

   d. _____

   e. _____

2. Who discovered this river? _____

3. In which South American country does it originate?

   _____

B. Read the entry for <u>Paris, France</u>.

1. On which river is this city located? _____

2. Who first settled in this area? _____

3. Name three things you would see if you visited Paris.

   _____

C. Read the entry for <u>Krakatau</u>.

1. What is another name for Krakatau? _____

2. Name a country near Krakatau. _____

3. When did Krakatau last erupt? _____

4. What was special about this eruption? _____

   _____

I. M. A. Booksnoop reproducible page, copyright © 1983

NAME _____

Geographical Dictionary Test

A. Read each statement below. Write *true* or *false* next to each one.

_____ 1. The geographical dictionary has an index.

_____ 2. Entries are listed alphabetically in the geographical dictionary.

_____ 3. Only the largest cities are listed.

_____ 4. The entry may give you some information about the history of the place.

_____ 5. Many places in the world have the same names.

_____ 6. This dictionary gives information about peninsulas and large mountains.

_____ 7. This dictionary has lists of the longest rivers, the highest mountains, and the largest cities.

_____ 8. The main reason for using the geographical dictionary is to study the maps.

_____ 9. Famous explorers are mentioned in this dictionary but are not listed as entries.

_____ 10. It is not unusual for a place to have two names.

B. Read the entry for <u>Hawaii</u>.

1. How many square miles does the island of Hawaii (the Big Island)

cover? _____

2. What is the largest city on the island of Hawaii? _____

3. Who was the first English explorer to visit the Hawaiian Islands?

_____

4. What was the former name of the Hawaiian Islands? _____

_____

5. When did Hawaii become a state? _____

I. M. A. Booksnoop reproducible page, copyright © 1983

The Geographical Dictionary 115

Teacher's Notes and Answer Keys

Booksnoop Pretest. pages 6—8

OBJECTIVE The students will demonstrate their knowledge of the uses of a library and of reference books.

SUGGESTIONS FOR USE The pretest is three pages long. The results of the pretest will guide you in preparing the appropriate lessons for your students. Students with a strong background will be able to function more independently and may benefit from a contract or learning-center approach to many of the activities in *Booksnoop*.

ANSWERS
A. **1.** 5, 4, 2, 1, 3 **2.** 1, 2, 4, 5, 3
B. **2, 3, 5, 6,** *and* **7** *should be circled.*
C. **1.** camera **2.** Pueblo **3.** Alexander the Great **4.** antibiotics **5.** Alabama
D. **1.** false **2.** true **3.** true **4.** true **5.** false
E. **1.** e **2.** a **3.** d **4.** f **5.** f **6.** c **7.** b **8.** c *or* e **9.** g **10.** b
F. **1.** false **2.** true **3.** false **4.** true **5.** true **6.** true **7.** false **8.** true **9.** true
   10. false

Unit I: Alphabet Sleuth

How to Be a Detective. page 13

OBJECTIVE The students will refresh their knowledge of alphabetizing and the use of guide words.

SUGGESTIONS FOR USE Make a transparency of this page and use it for reviewing or reteaching alphabetizing and guide word usage. In question A-4, bring to your students' attention the fact that two-part entries follow alphabetizing rules. In other words, *coaster* comes before *coast guard* because *e* comes before *g*. In part B, point out that a person is listed by the last name and that a geographical feature is listed by the main part of its name. *Mount Rushmore* would be under *R*, but *Mount Vernon* would be under *M* because it is a city.

ANSWERS
A. **1.** Alabama **2.** motorcade **3.** rhinestone **4.** coaster **5.** microbe
B. **1.** Andrew Bailey **2.** Samuel, Aaron **3.** Mount Everest *(under* E) **4.** Amazon
   River **5.** George Washington Carver
C. **1.** before **2.** after **3.** before **4.** on **5.** after **6.** after **7.** after **8.** on
   9. on **10.** on

Alphabet Clues. page 14

OBJECTIVE The students will demonstrate their knowledge of the alphabet and their ability to put words into alphabetical order.

SUGGESTIONS FOR USE Use this page as a transparency or as a student worksheet. The alphabetizing section of the pretest will help you decide how much review your students need. As a follow-up activity, have the students prepare lists of words for friends to alphabetize.

ANSWERS
A. **1.** c, d, e **2.** n, o, p **3.** e, f, g **4.** m, n, o **5.** t, u, v **6.** x, y, z **7.** d, e, f
8. j, k, l **9.** f, g, h **10.** v, w, x **11.** i, j, k **12.** q, r, s
B. **1.** 3, 1, 4, 2, 5 **2.** 4, 3, 1, 5, 2 **3.** 1, 2, 3, 4, 5
C. **1.** straight, i, n **2.** Pluto, o, n **3.** egoism, y, o **4.** mosaic, a, q **5.** Alabama, b, m
6. cycle, o, e **7.** whale, a, e **8.** rodent, n, o **9.** victory, d, c **10.** brazen, e, i

Name Sleuth. page 15

OBJECTIVE The students will demonstrate their ability to alphabetize names.

SUGGESTIONS FOR USE Use this page as a warm-up exercise for Unit 9, The Encyclopedia, or Unit 10, The Biographical Dictionary. Use the alphabetizing or names section of the transparency master to determine how much review your students need. Discuss the application of alphabetizing concepts to the telephone directory. If you need to prepare more written practice for your group, use your local telephone directory as source material.

ANSWERS
A. 2, 6, 9, 1, 5, 4, 10, 7, 3, 8
B. 3, 7, 10, 8, 6, 1, 4, 9, 5, 2
C. 7, 6, 9, 1, 3, 4, 8, 10, 2, 5

The Detective's Assistant. page 16

OBJECTIVE The students will demonstrate their ability to use guide words.

SUGGESTIONS FOR USE Guide word use requires high-level alphabetizing skills. Most reference books have guide words. Being able to use guide words makes locating entries easier. If the guide word section of the pretest indicated your students are rusty in this area, make a transparency of this page and use it as a directed lesson.

ANSWERS
A. Marianas Islands, Maria Theresa, mare, Marburg, March, margarine
B. *Accept any reasonable definition.*

Investigating Guide Words. page 17

OBJECTIVE The students will demonstrate their ability to use guide words.

SUGGESTIONS FOR USE Discuss the concepts presented on the page. Explain the directions for part A. Part C may be eliminated when you reproduce this page.

ANSWERS
A. **1.** on **2.** before **3.** after **4.** on **5.** on **6.** on **7.** on **8.** after **9.** before
10. after
B. **1.** Clay, Henry **3.** Cicero **5.** Churchill, Winston **7.** Charles I **8.** Cato **9.** Clark, George R.
C. 9, 2, 7, 3, 6, 1, 5, 4, 8, 10

Guide Word Graduate. page 18

OBJECTIVE The students will demonstrate their ability to use guide words.

SUGGESTIONS FOR USE The activity reinforces the skills introduced on pages 16 and 17.

ANSWERS
  A. **1.** Santiago **4.** Santa Fe **7.** Scilly Isles **10.** Scipio **11.** Schubert, Franz **12.** Saxony
  B. **1.** on **2.** before **3.** after **4.** on **5.** before **6.** after **7.** on **8.** on **9.** on **10.** after **11.** on **12.** on **13.** before **14.** after **15.** before **16.** on
  C. checkers, cheese, chemical, chetah, Cheyenne, chic, Chicago, Chickasaw, chicle, Chief of Staff, chieftain, child, chimney, chipmunk, chlorine, chrome

Alphabet Sleuth Test. page 19

OBJECTIVE The students will demonstrate their alphabetizing skills and their ability to use guide words.

SUGGESTIONS FOR USE Use the test results to plan for reviewing and reteaching.

ANSWERS
  A. **1.** 6, 4, 1, 2, 5, 3, 7, 8 **2.** 1, 3, 2, 6, 5, 4, 7, 8
  B. **1.** Winchester **2.** Weddell **7.** Westchester **8.** Whitehorse **9.** West Indies **11.** Waterford **12.** White Nile **13.** Washington

Unit 2: Parts of a Book

Background Information

The typical nonfiction book does not contain all of the items listed below. However, as your more able students may ask you about them, the list is comprehensive.

Acknowledgements: The author thanks the people who made contributions to the book. Acknowledgements are usually found in the front of the book.

Appendix: Usually found in the back of a book, this section gives details that elucidate the main body of information. Charts, maps, tables, and statistics are often found in an appendix.

Bibliography: There are two types of bibliographies. The first type lists books or articles that the author used to prepare the book. The second type lists books that the author recommends for further reading. Both listings are alphabetical, usually by the authors' names.

Copyright: The copyright is the legal right conferred by the United States Register of Copyrights to the author or publisher. It gives exclusive control over the book to the author or publisher. The date of copyright and the International Standard Book Number (ISBN) are given on the back of the title page.

Dedication: This page usually follows the copyright page. The author thanks someone who or something that inspired or influenced the writing of the book.

Foreword: This section is usually written by someone other than the author and is located after the table of contents. It gives a general statement about the intent or content of the book.

Glossary: This section is located in the back of a book. It is a dictionary of special terms relevant to the book's content.

Half title page: This page precedes the title page and tells only the title of the book.

Index: This section is usually located in the back of a book. It lists items alphabetically with their page numbers. Lists of maps and illustrations may be included in an index.

Introduction: This section is usually found just before the main text. It often gives background information to introduce the content. It may serve as a preface and may be written by someone other than the author.

List of illustrations or maps: This section lists pictures, diagrams, or maps with their page numbers for quick reference. It may be included in the book's index or with the table of contents.

Preface: This section is usually found prior to or just after the table of contents. It states the author's intent in writing the book.

Table of contents: This section is located after the title page. It is a list of the sections or chapters of a book, in the order in which they appear, with the corresponding page numbers.

Title page: This page may be the first page in a book. It lists the book's full title, the author's name, the publisher, and the place of publication. It may also include the name of a translator, an illustrator, a designer, or an editor.

There Are Two Sides to Every Story. page 24

OBJECTIVE The students will become familiar with the information given on a typical title page and with copyright information.

SUGGESTIONS FOR USE This page may be used as a transparency for a teacher-directed activity or as a student worksheet. As a follow-up activity, have your students locate the title pages of the textbooks they are using. Question #7 should be discussed thoroughly. The type of information you need determines how current the book's copyright needs to be. Make your students aware that the current almanac is an up-to-date source of statistics.

ANSWERS
1. Eric Dalton 2. Land of Many Cultures 3. Fairfield Publishers 4. New York
5. Margaret Batesford 6. 1975 7. *Answers will vary. It will depend on the type of information you need.* 8. 0–603–02437–1

Sifting for Big Clues: The Table of Contents, page 25

OBJECTIVE The students will demonstrate their knowledge of the scope and limitations of a typical table of contents.

SUGGESTIONS FOR USE This page may be used as a transparency or as a student worksheet. Many students turn to the table of contents when the index should be used. Discuss the answers to questions B-4 and B-8 to contrast reasons for using the table of contents with reasons for using the index.

ANSWERS
A. 1. front 2. main ideas
B. 1. The Rise of the Aztecs 2. 10 3. 8 4. 2 5. glossary 6. index

Sifting for Clues: Using the Index pages 26–27

OBJECTIVE The students will demonstrate their ability to locate information in a typical index.

SUGGESTIONS FOR USE Duplicate copies of page 26 for each student. Make a transparency of the page to use as an introduction to using an index if the pretest indicated a major weakness in this area. Page 26 is also used to complete page 27. The following concepts should be discussed: Indexes are alphabetical; there are main topics and subtopics; this index uses an asterisk to indicate an illustration, but there are other ways to do so; an item may be listed under more than one topic, and some indexes have a "see also" reference; the dash between page numbers means "through." Discuss the answers to page 26 before handing out page 27.

ANSWERS
A. 1. 46 2. 82 3. 41 and 47 4. 52 5. 42, 49, and 60 6. 64 7. 40
B. 6, 8, 3, 4, 5, 2, 7, 1
C. 1. 36, 42, 52 2. 42, 47, 58 3. 55 4. 40, 50, 42, 47, 49, 58, 60 5. 52 6. 189
   7. 92–93
D. 1. alphabetically 2. The index gives the exact location of a specific item. 3. It uses an asterisk *(or italics or other device)*. 4. The dash means "through." 5. The index helps you locate details, but the table of contents tells you only the main ideas.

The Informer: The Bibliography. page 28

OBJECTIVE The students will demonstrate their knowledge of a typical bibliography.

SUGGESTIONS FOR USE Discuss the reasons for using a bibliography in a textbook: It tells you the references the author used in compiling the information and it gives you references for further study. Have your students locate the bibliographies in their classroom textbooks.

ANSWERS
A. **1.** back   **2.** It can tell you where to find more information. It tells you how up-to-date the author's sources were.   **3.** alphabetically by the authors' last names
B. **1.** Hayman   **2.** Caulfred   **3.** Caulfred *(The other books are primarily historical and are less likely to have out-of-date information.)*   **4.** Allred, Emery, Hayman
5. Frankfort   **6.** Lernan   **7.** Emery   **8.** Allred, Emery

Parts of a Book Test. pages 29–30

OBJECTIVE The students will demonstrate their knowledge of and ability to use a title page, a table of contents, an index, and a bibliography.

SUGGESTIONS FOR USE Administer this test after your students have completed the activities in the unit. The ability to use an index is critical to reference-book use. Reteach if the test indicates weaknesses in the use of an index.

ANSWERS
A. **1.** a **2.** b **3.** c **4.** d **5.** e **6.** c **7.** e **8.** a **9.** d **10.** a
B. **1.** false **2.** true **3.** true **4.** true **5.** true
C. **1.** 37–42 **2.** 29, 32–35 **3.** 192–195 **4.** social structure **5.** 192–195
6. 55–56 **7.** 196–203 **8.** 30–33

Unit 3: The Dewey Decimal System

Background Information

The Dewey Decimal System of book classification is used by most libraries in the United States except the Library of Congress. Nonfiction books are arranged according to their Dewey Decimal System call numbers. All books bearing the same call number are further classified alphabetically by the authors' last names. If one author has written several books on the same topic, the books are alphabetized by title. Biographies are arranged alphabetically by the name of the person the book is about. Several biographies about the same person are further arranged by the authors' last names. Fiction books do not have call numbers and are identified by an *F* on their spines. They are placed in a separate section and are arranged by the authors' last names. Books by the same author are arranged alphabetically by their titles.

See page 37 for the Dewey Decimal System classification chart.

Where Is It? page 35

OBJECTIVE The students will become familiar with the Dewey Decimal System of classifying books.

SUGGESTIONS FOR USE Make a transparency of this page and use it to introduce your students to the Dewey Decimal System. Discuss terms that may not be in your students' vocabularies, such as *philosophy* and *technology*. If you are conducting this lesson in your classroom, make a map of your school library showing the locations of the categories. Arrange a trip to a local public library as a follow-up. If there is a large city or college library nearby, arrange a visit. Many of your students will be astounded at the materials available in a comprehensive library. A library should become a friendly place to your students if they are to feel comfortable and self-motivated enough to use it.

ANSWERS
- **A.** **1.** General Works (references, usually cannot be checked out) **2.** Philosophy **3.** Religion **4.** Social Sciences **5.** Language **6.** Pure Science **7.** Technology **8.** Arts **9.** Literature **10.** History. *(See Looking for Clues, p. 37, for a more complete description of each category.)*
- **B.** 4, 3, 1, 2, 5

Following Leads. page 36

OBJECTIVE The students will locate the Dewey Decimal System sections in their library.

SUGGESTIONS FOR USE This worksheet must be completed in a library. If you do not have a school library, make a list of call numbers, titles, and authors on a transparency and have the students complete the worksheet with this information. Better yet, plan a trip to a local library. Make a map of the library and use it to prepare your group for the trip.

ANSWERS *Answers will vary. Have your students share the names of the books that they find especially interesting.*

Looking for Clues. page 37

OBJECTIVE The students will demonstrate their knowledge of the Dewey Decimal System.

SUGGESTIONS FOR USE Discuss the subtopics before assigning this page. The 600s, Technology, may need further explanation.

ANSWERS
- **1.** 400–499 **2.** 900–999 **3.** 600–699 **4.** 500–599 **5.** 700–799 **6.** 800–899 **7.** 300–399 **8.** 700–799 **9.** 700–799 **10.** 000–099 **11.** 200–299 **12.** 100–199

Remembering the Clues. page 38

OBJECTIVE The students will construct mnemonics to remember the Dewey Decimal System of classification.

SUGGESTIONS FOR USE A mnemonic device is an artificial memory aid. After the students make theirs, have volunteers read them aloud. Choose the best one and have your group memorize it.

ANSWERS
- **A.** Mechanics prepare many Venus expeditions, never using strange jalopies.
- **B.** *Answers will vary.*

Dewey Decimal System Test. page 39

OBJECTIVE The students will demonstrate their understanding of the Dewey Decimal System of classification.

SUGGESTIONS FOR USE Administer the test when the activities in this unit have been satisfactorily completed. Review the use of the Dewey Decimal System periodically.

ANSWERS
- **1.** 900 **2.** 400 **3.** 700 **4.** 200 **5.** 100 **6.** 600 **7.** 000 **8.** 800 **9.** 700 **10.** 900

Unit 4: The Card Catalog

Tracing the Cards. page 44

OBJECTIVE The students will complete author, title, and subject catalog cards for a given book.

SUGGESTIONS FOR USE Make a transparency of this page and use it to review or introduce the three types of catalog cards. Most students will not be able to complete this activity without teacher direction. Duplicate copies of this page and have your students complete it as you lead them using the overhead projector. Make up your own book information and use this page for review at a later time.

ANSWERS

1. subject card

```
        TENNIS
 786
  G     Gonzales, Erica
          Winning at tennis. Illus by Janet Winslow.
        Brownsville Publishers 1982    176p illus.
```

2. title card

```
        Winning at tennis
 786
  G     Gonzales, Erica
          Winning at tennis. Illus by Janet Winslow.
        Brownsville Publishers 1982    176p illus.
```

3. author card

```
 786
  G     Gonzales, Erica
          Winning at tennis. Illus by Janet Winslow
        Brownsville Publishers 1982    176p illus.
```

Tracing the Trays. page 45

OBJECTIVE The students will become familiar with the card catalog.

SUGGESTIONS FOR USE If this is your students' first exposure to the card catalog, make a transparency of this page and duplicate copies for your class. Have your students complete the worksheet under your guidance.

ANSWERS

A. 1. 14 **2.** 1 **3.** 9 **4.** 1 **5.** 3
B. 1. 4 **2.** 9 **3.** 7 **4.** 8 **5.** 14 **6.** 12 **7.** 9 **8.** 12
C. 1. 4 **2.** 8 **3.** 7 **4.** 6 **5.** 7

Clues in the Trays. page 46

OBJECTIVE The students will use this card catalog to find specific information.

SUGGESTIONS FOR USE This activity requires a card catalog. Assign each student a card catalog tray. Have the students note that the card catalog uses guide words to assist in the quick location of cards. Instead of checking each assignment, conduct a class discussion about interesting subjects, titles, and favorite authors listed in the card catalog.

ANSWERS *Answers will vary.*

Clues in the Cards. page 47

OBJECTIVE The students will demonstrate their understanding of the information found on the three types of cards in a card catalog.

SUGGESTIONS FOR USE Your students should have no difficulty completing this worksheet. Use this activity as an informal pretest for the unit test.

ANSWERS
  A. **1.** subject **2.** 636.7 Mc **3.** Mc
  B. **1.** author **2.** Odin and His Family **3.** Robert Closse
  C. **1.** title **2.** fiction section **3.** George Knobb

Unscramble the Clues. page 48

OBJECTIVE The students will complete the three types of catalog cards for a given book.

SUGGESTIONS FOR USE Use the transparency you made to introduce this unit as a review before making this assignment if you think your group will have difficulty.

ANSWERS
  1.

	EGYPT
932 F	Fowler, Kenneth
	Life in ancient egypt. Illus by Marg. Boehmer.
	Scribner Publishers 1975 164p illus.

  2.

	Life in ancient egypt
932 F	Fowler, Kenneth
	Life in ancient egypt. Illus by Marg. Boehmer.
	Scribner Publishers 1975 164p illus.

  3.

932 F	Fowler, Kenneth
	Life in ancient egypt. Illus by Marg. Boehmer.
	Scribner Publishers 1975 164p illus.

Card Catalog Test. page 49

OBJECTIVE The students will demonstrate their knowledge of the card catalog.

SUGGESTIONS FOR USE Use the test results to determine necessary reteaching.

ANSWERS
- **A.** author, title, subject
- **B.** **1.** The Gold Rush Days **2.** Sarah H. Abbott **3.** 1965 **4.** 976.6 A **5.** Goldstone
- **C.**

```
┌────────────────────────────────────────────────────────────┐
│     Mystery of the missing computer                          │
│                                                              │
│     Morrison, Nancy                                          │
│       Mystery of the missing computer. Illus. by Jerry Smith.│
│     Weldon Publishing 1983    138p illus.                    │
└────────────────────────────────────────────────────────────┘
```

Unit 5: The Thesaurus

Crime Stopper. page 54

OBJECTIVE The students will become familiar with the structure of a thesaurus.

SUGGESTIONS FOR USE Make an overhead transparency of this page and use it to introduce your students to the organization of a thesaurus patterned after *Roget's International Thesaurus.* Other types of synonym dictionaries list the words alphabetically and are simpler to use. Include the following points in your discussion:

1. The thesaurus is a tool to improve the students' writing.
2. It assumes you know the meaning of the word.
3. To find a synonym or an antonym for a word, find the word in the index. Choose the meaning that fits the context of the word. Find the entry number for the meaning and turn to its location.
4. Words are listed in categories. Your word may not be a main entry, so skim the category to find it.

Sailing by Thesaurus. page 55

OBJECTIVE The students will use the thesaurus to find synonyms for words.

SUGGESTIONS FOR USE Familiarize your students with the organizational pattern of your classroom thesauruses. If you have a limited number of copies, make this worksheet an activity center.

ANSWERS *(Answers will vary according to your classroom thesauruses. These answers are keyed to* Roget's.*)*
- **A.** *Accept any interpretation of* good.
- **B.** *Possible answers are:* **1.** voyage, passage **2.** wages, compensation **3.** withstand, battle **4.** inhospitable, unagreeable **5.** capsized, upset **6.** violent, furious **7.** energy, power **8.** stationary, riding at anchor **9.** consequence, outcome **10.** prolonged, extended *(A group discussion of the individual choices would be a valuable way to complete this activity.)*

Finding the Rhyme for Us Using a Thesaurus. page 56

OBJECTIVE The students will use a thesaurus to locate synonyms that rhyme with clue words.

SUGGESTIONS FOR USE Approach this as a fun activity. Browsing through the thesaurus will make your students feel more comfortable with the reference book.

ANSWERS **1.** maim *or* lame **2.** abhor **3.** collide **4.** loquacious **5.** subdue **6.** propitious *or* auspicious **7.** garble **8.** vigor **9.** sinister **10.** lurk **11.** sham **12.** notion **13.** probe **14.** heed **15.** quest **16.** remorse **17.** foe **18.** gaunt **19.** hue

The Thesaurus Goes to the Movies. page 57

OBJECTIVE The students will categorize words using a thesaurus.

SUGGESTIONS FOR USE Have the students locate the Synopsis of Categories section if they are using *Roget's*. Check answers through class discussion.

ANSWERS
Light — emanation, fluorescent, gleam, glimmer, glint, glow, illumination, lucence, luminary, luminescence, luminous, luster, radiance, sheen
Sound — acoustics, intonation, monotone, noise, pitch, report, sonance, sonic, soniferous, timbre, tonality, tonation, tone, tonic
Motion — activity, actuation, budge, dynamic, flow, flux, kinesis, mobilization, motor, movableness, movement, ongoing, stir, travel

Thesaurus Test. page 58

OBJECTIVE The students will demonstrate their mastery of the use of a thesaurus.

SUGGESTIONS FOR USE Administer this test when your students have completed the activities in the unit. The test requires the use of a thesaurus.

ANSWERS
A. 1. false **2.** false **3.** true **4.** false **5.** true
B. and **C.** *Accept any answers that are synonyms for the given words.*

Unit 6: The Atlas

Your Travel Guide: The Atlas. page 63

OBJECTIVE The students will become familiar with a typical table of contents and an index for an atlas.

SUGGESTIONS FOR USE Compare your classroom atlases with the information on this page. Make a transparency and use it to introduce your group to using the atlas. It may be necessary to familiarize your students with new terms, such as *political, physical,* and *natural vegetation*. Introduce them to the abbreviations found in an atlas. The abbreviations used on the transparency master are *C.* for "cape," *R.* for "river," *Nat'l Mon.* for "national monument," *Is.* for "island," *Lat.* for "latitude," *Long.* for "longitude," and common abbreviations of names of states, countries, and continents. Have your students explore the contents and indexes in the classroom atlases as a conclusion to your presentation.

Getting Acquainted. page 64

OBJECTIVE The students will use the table of contents in an atlas to locate specific maps.

SUGGESTIONS FOR USE Compare the atlases you are using with the worksheet. Explain any terms on the worksheet that are not compatible with your atlases. If your supply of atlases is limited, have the students work in pairs.

ANSWERS *Answers will vary with the atlases being used.*

Making Conversation. page 65

OBJECTIVE The students will use the index of an atlas to locate listings of cities.

SUGGESTIONS FOR USE Your classroom atlases may use a grid system for locating specific map items (for example, *A6*). If so, change the worksheet to correspond. If your atlases give pronunciations too, point out this added help.

ANSWERS *(Latitudes and longitudes are given. Consult the atlases being used for page numbers.)*
   A. **1.** 38 N, 23 E **2.** 46 N, 7 E **3.** 30 N, 31 E **4.** 43 N, 79 W **5.** 38 N, 77 W **6.** 19 N, 99 W **7.** 16 S, 68 W **8.** 33 S, 151 E **9.** 22 N, 88 E **10.** 37 N, 127 E **11.** 33 N, 44 E **12.** 22 N, 96 E **13.** 39 N, 32 E **14.** 10 N, 66 W **15.** 1 S, 37 E
   B. *Answers will vary.*

Being Neighborly. page 66

OBJECTIVE The students will use a table of contents and maps to identify countries that border given countries.

SUGGESTIONS FOR USE Your students must be able to identify borders of countries as indicated on the maps in their atlases. Have them practice finding the neighboring countries of some places not on the worksheet. Use countries that are currently in the news.

ANSWERS *(Page numbers will vary.)*
   1. Italy, Switzerland, West Germany, Luxemburg, Belgium, Spain, Monaco, Andorra
   2. Norway, Finland **3.** Austria, Yugoslavia, Romania, Soviet Union, Czechoslovakia
   4. Algeria, Niger, Chad, Sudan, Egypt, Tunisia **5.** Saudi Arabia, Jordan, Syria, Turkey, Iran, Kuwait **6.** Guatemala, Honduras **7.** Brazil, Paraguay, Argentina, Chile, Peru
   8. Afghanistan, Pakistan, China, Nepal, Bhutan, Bangladesh, Burma **9.** United States, Guatemala, Belize

Atlas Test. page 67

OBJECTIVE The students will demonstrate their understanding of the correct uses of an atlas.

SUGGESTIONS FOR USE Read this worksheet before you administer the test to be sure the major concepts have been covered.

ANSWERS
   A. *Answers will vary.*
   B. **1.** 1, 5, 3, 4, 2 **2.** 1, 5, 4, 3, 2

Unit 7: Bartlett's Familiar Quotations

Meet Mr. Bartlett. page 72

OBJECTIVE The students will become familiar with the indexing system and the form of a typical entry in a book of quotations.

SUGGESTIONS FOR USE Make a transparency of this page and use it to introduce books of quotations. Point out the use of commas in the index and the helpful guide words at the tops of the pages. The index of quotations in Bartlett's does not include authors' names. Check the books of quotations you have available and introduce your students to their indexing methods. Your students should be made aware of the footnotes used to mention quotations that are related to the one given. Discuss the use of a key word in the quotation in locating it in the index. Identify the key words *pup, dog,* and *nose* in your discussion.

Getting in Step with Bartlett. page 73

OBJECTIVE The students will construct an index from the given quotations.

SUGGESTIONS FOR USE This worksheet does not require the use of a book of quotations. Students will benefit from the indexing practice.

ANSWERS 1. 3, 5, 1, 4, 2 **2.** 5, 1, 4, 2, 3 **3.** 2, 1, 3, 5, 4 **4.** 4, 1, 3, 2, 5

Who Said That? page 74

OBJECTIVE The students will use Bartlett's *Familiar Quotations* to locate the authors of given lines.

SUGGESTIONS FOR USE This worksheet is keyed to Bartlett's. Your more able students may enjoy using the *Oxford Book of Quotations* or the *Home Book of Quotations*. Tell them that some of the quotations will not be found in those references. If you think your students are not able to identify the key word in a quotation, do this as a group activity.

ANSWERS 1. Edgar Allan Poe **2.** James Whitcomb Riley **3.** Aesop **4.** Henry David Thoreau **5.** Samuel Taylor Coleridge **6.** Charles Dickens **7.** Ralph Waldo Emerson **8.** Washington Irving **9.** Joyce Kilmer **10.** Ogden Nash

The Case of the Interrupted Quotation. page 75

OBJECTIVE The students will use Bartlett's *Familiar Quotations* to complete quotations.

SUGGESTIONS FOR USE Your students should experience little difficulty completing this activity. You may need to define *stanza*.

ANSWERS 1. and two if by sea; And I on the opposite shore will be, / Ready to ride and spread the alarm / Through every Middlesex village and farm. **2.** Yo-ho-ho, and a bottle of rum! / Drink and the devil had done for the rest— / Yo-ho-ho, and a bottle of rum! **3.** In the forests of the night, / What immortal hand or eye / Could frame thy fearful symmetry? **4.** Loved the wood-rose, / and left it on its stalk? **5.** to forgive divine. **6.** our fearful trip is done! / The ship has weather'd every rack, the prize we sought is won, / The port is near, the bells I hear, the people all exulting.

Bartlett's Test. page 76

OBJECTIVE The students will demonstrate their ability to use Bartlett's.

SUGGESTIONS FOR USE When the activities in this unit have been completed, administer this test. Reteach if test results indicate weaknesses.

ANSWERS
A. **1.** true **2.** false **3.** true **4.** false **5.** false
B. *(Several answers are correct for each quotation. Accept any correct one.)* **1.** serve, stand, wait **2.** books, tasted, swallowed, digested **3.** fools, angels **4.** happy, house, friend **5.** three, secret **6.** reward **7.** rose **8.** love, wall **9.** day's, work **10.** wishes, horses, beggers, ride

Unit 8: The Almanac

Using the Fact Locator. page 81

OBJECTIVE The students will demonstrate their understanding of a typical almanac index.

SUGGESTIONS FOR USE Make a transparency of the page and use it to initiate a class discussion about the peculiarities of an almanac index. Information about a topic is often distributed throughout the almanac. The students should have little difficulty answering the questions on the second part of this transparency.

ANSWERS
A. **1.** 687 **2.** 420 **3.** 356 **4.** 488 **5.** 712–713 **6.** not answerable **7.** 434
8. 259
B. **1.** freight **2.** longest *or* United States **3.** inventions **4.** population

Which Department? page 82

OBJECTIVE The students will determine which questions are best answered by an almanac.

SUGGESTIONS FOR USE Use this activity to introduce your students to the almanac. Advances in technology and science, sports records, statistics of the economies of nations, facts about persons of prominence, awards given, and political developments of the year are types of information included in a typical almanac. The better known almanacs are the *New York Times Almanac,* the *Information Please Almanac,* and the *World Almanac.* Part B of this activity requires the use of an almanac.

ANSWERS
A. *(Answers may vary. Accept other reasonable answers.)* **1.** yes **2.** yes **3.** yes
4. encyclopedia **5.** yes **6.** yes **7.** encyclopedia **8.** yes
B. *Answers will vary.*

Department, Please! page 83

OBJECTIVE The students will determine topics indexed in an almanac and use the almanac to answer questions.

SUGGESTIONS FOR USE Determining index topics is the key to using an almanac easily. Discuss the answers thoroughly with your group. If your supply of almanacs is limited, part B can be completed on an individual basis at a later time.

ANSWERS
A. **1.** baseball **2.** weather *or* space **3.** inventions **4.** automobiles **5.** United
Nations **6.** South Africa **7.** weather **8.** coffee **9.** automobiles **10.** Saturn
B. *Answers will vary.*

Only the Facts, Please! page 84

OBJECTIVE The students will use the almanac to write questions and answers for given topics.

SUGGESTIONS FOR USE This worksheet can become a game after it is completed. Check the questions the students have written for appropriateness first. Then divide the group into four or more teams. One person from each team sits on the answer panel. A student asks a question and the panel members compete to be the first to answer the question and earn points for the team.

ANSWERS *Answers will vary. Be sure the questions apply to the given topic.*

Almanac Test, page 85

OBJECTIVE The students will demonstrate their understanding of the use and limitations of an almanac.

SUGGESTIONS FOR USE Administer this test when you feel your group is ready. Provide more hands-on time for those students who score poorly.

ANSWERS

   A. **1.** yes **2.** no **3.** no **4.** no **5.** yes **6.** yes **7.** no **8.** no **9.** yes **10.** yes

   B. **1.** animals **2.** oil *or* petroleum **3.** Lincoln, Abraham **4.** lakes **5.** automobiles *or* racing

Unit 9: The Encyclopedia

Finding the Keys. page 91

OBJECTIVE The students will determine the key word to use to locate the answer to a specific question in an encyclopedia.

SUGGESTIONS FOR USE Make a transparency of this activity. Include the following points as you identify the key words in part A: A key word is the main entry you would use to find the fact that will answer the question; knowing the key word in a research question will save time. For part B, explain what a cross-reference is. Point out the two usual locations for an encyclopedia's index: the back of each volume or a separate volume.

ANSWERS

   A. **1.** barometer **2.** Incas **3.** gasoline **4.** dodo **5.** helicopter **6.** knight **7.** plastics **8.** light **9.** knot **10.** immunity

   B. **1.** b **2.** c **3.** d **4.** e **5.** a

Using the Keys. page 92

OBJECTIVE The students will find five facts about a given topic in an encyclopedia.

SUGGESTIONS FOR USE Assign one of the topics in part B to each student, or allow students to choose their own. There is a topic for each letter of the alphabet. The ability to recognize main ideas and note-taking skills are stressed in this assignment. Eliminate part D if you do not wish your students to write the paragraph.

ANSWERS

   A. The copyright date tells how up-to-date the information will be.

   B and **C.** *Answers will vary.*

Who Did It? page 93

OBJECTIVE The students will demonstrate their ability to locate information in an encyclopedia.

SUGGESTIONS FOR USE Part A reviews finding names. Part B reviews finding specific items. Since part B contains thirty items, make it an open-ended assignment by setting a minimum for the less able students and encouraging the more highly able ones to find as many as possible. The items are spread out through the alphabet to maximize the use of your encyclopedias.

ANSWERS

   A. **1.** T **2.** G **3.** D **4.** E **5.** W **6.** G

   B. **1.** Pascal **2.** Carrier **3.** Volta **4.** Otis **5.** Ritty **6.** Nobel **7.** Brayton, Daimler **8.** Geiger **9.** Starley **10.** Brewster **11.** Daimler **12.** Mége-Mouriz **13.** Blanchard

Discover the Details. pages 94–95

OBJECTIVE The students will use the encyclopedia to research given topics.

SUGGESTIONS FOR USE This activity contains 20 research projects. Most of the projects do not require large amounts of writing. Again, topics are spread throughout the alphabet to allow maximum use of the available encyclopedias.

Encyclopedia Test. page 96

OBJECTIVE The students will demonstrate their knowledge of the scope and limitations of an encyclopedia.

SUGGESTIONS FOR USE Administer this test after the students have completed the activities in this unit.

ANSWERS
 A. **1.** false **2.** true **3.** false **4.** true **5.** true
 B. **1.** moon, M **2.** elements, E **3.** calendar, C **4.** antiseptics, A **5.** Alaska, A
 6. plants, P **7.** French and Indian War, F **8.** eclipse, E **9.** Marco Polo, P **10.** King Henry VIII, H

Unit 10: The Biographical Dictionary

Biographical Dictionary Page. page 102

OBJECTIVE The students will become familiar with a typical biographical dictionary page.

SUGGESTIONS FOR USE Make an overhead of this page from *Webster's Biographical Dictionary.* Use it to introduce your group to the biographical dictionary. Since most libraries have limited copies of this reference, the other activities can be presented as activity centers. Include the following points in your discussion:
 1. Names are listed alphabetically.
 2. Refer to the *Thomas Jefferson* entry to show that information is limited to the highlights of a person's career.
 3. Refer to the entry for *Jehan* to show that variant spellings are not unusual.
 4. Have the students note the dates during which some of the people entered on this page lived to show the scope of the biographical dictionary.
 5. Review how your particular biographical dictionaries list people whose names begin with *Mc* and *Mac*.

Who Am I? page 103

OBJECTIVE The students will locate specific information about people in the biographical dictionary.

SUGGESTIONS FOR USE If your supply of biographical dictionaries is limited, make this worksheet an activity center. Paul Zindel may not be listed in your biographical dictionary. Challenge your students to go to another reference book to discover what he did.

ANSWERS
 A. **1.** 1864–1943, uses for peanuts **2.** 1860–1961, paintings **3.** 1840–1921, pneumatic tire **4.** 1881–1958, motion picture company **5.** 1846–1914, air brake
 6. 1881–1955, penicillin **7.** 1738–1822, Uranus **8.** 1878–1968, protoactinium
 9. 1867–1934, polonium and radium **10.** 1849–1926, Burbank potato
 B. **1.** *Under the Sea Wind* or *Silent Spring* **2.** *Tarzan of the Apes* **3.** *The Good Earth*
 4. *The Effect of Gamma Rays on Man-in-the-Moon Marigolds* **5.** *A Street in Bronzeville*

Aliases. page 104

OBJECTIVE The students will use the biographical dictionary to locate pseudonyms or nicknames and careers of famous people.

SUGGESTIONS FOR USE Many famous people are more well known by their pseudonyms or nicknames than by their given names. You may wish to introduce this activity by having the students guess who some of the people are. Make this worksheet an activity center if your supply of biographical dictionaries is limited.

ANSWERS 1. Babe Ruth or the Bambino, baseball player **2.** Mark Twain, author **3.** Isaac Bickerstaff, author **4.** Eric Weiss, magician **5.** El Greco, painter **6.** Mahatma Gandhi, Indian nationalist leader **7.** Buffalo Bill, American scout and showman **8.** Light-Horse Harry Lee, American soldier and statesman **9.** The Lady with the Lamp, English nurse and hospital reformer **10.** Billy the Kid, American desperado **11.** The Commoner, lawyer and political leader **12.** George Eliot, author **13.** Angelo G. Roncalli, Roman Catholic leader **14.** Mad Anthony, American Revolutionary officer **15.** Maid of Orleans, French national hero

How Are We Related? page 105

OBJECTIVE The students will use the biographical dictionary to determine the relationships of people.

SUGGESTIONS FOR USE If your supply of biographical dictionaries is limited, make this worksheet an activity center.

ANSWERS 1. artists **2.** scouts and guides **3.** inventors **4.** U.S. presidents **5.** composers **6.** American generals **7.** educators **8.** religious leaders

Biographical Dictionary Test. page 106

OBJECTIVE The students will demonstrate their knowledge of the biographical dictionary.

SUGGESTIONS FOR USE Administer this test when your students have completed the activities for this unit. Omit part B if you wish.

ANSWERS
  A. 1. true **2.** true **3.** false **4.** false **5.** false **6.** true **7.** true **8.** false
  B. *Answers will vary.*

Unit II: The Geographical Dictionary

Geographical Dictionary Page. page 111

OBJECTIVE The students will become familiar with the geographical dictionary.

SUGGESTIONS FOR USE Make a transparency of this page from *Webster's Geographical Dictionary*. Use it to introduce your group to this reference book. Include the following points in your discussion:
  1. Entries are alphabetical.
  2. The relative importance of a place determines the length of its entry. (See *Maryland*, for example.)
  3. Show how places with the same name are listed. (See *Marysville*.)
  4. Some places have more than one name. (See *Mary Island*.)
  5. Note the types of information given: geographical and historical.
  6. Discuss the usefulness of this book in finding basic facts about a place quickly.

Finding Your Way. page 112

OBJECTIVE The students will use a geographical dictionary to locate specific information.

SUGGESTIONS FOR USE If your supply of geographical dictionaries is limited, make this an activity center. Your students should have fun with question #7. We were surprised to find places named Prizzi and Hoffman!

1–9. *Answers will vary with the dictionary being used.* **10.** Washington **11.** green **12.** *Answers will vary.* **13.** Russia *or* Soviet Union **14.** Canada

Clues from First to Last. page 113

OBJECTIVE The students will use a geographical dictionary to solve riddles.

SUGGESTIONS FOR USE Use this worksheet as an activity center if your supply of geographical dictionaries is limited.

ANSWERS
1. Greenland **2.** Caspian Sea **3.** Nile River; 4,145 miles **4.** Dead Sea **5.** Vesuvius **6.** Sahara **7.** Angel Falls **8.** Easter Island **9.** Mount Rushmore

Get the Geographical Facts. page 114

OBJECTIVE The students will become familiar with entries for a river, a city, a geographical feature, and a state.

SUGGESTIONS FOR USE Make this worksheet an activity center if your supply of geographical dictionaries is limited. If you wish, have the students write their own questions about entries for others to answer.

ANSWERS
A. 1. *Answers will vary.* **2.** Pinzon **3.** Peru
B. 1. Seine **2.** Romans **3.** *Answers will vary.*
C. 1. Krakatoa **2.** Java **3.** August 27–28, 1883 **4.** It was the biggest volcanic eruption in recorded history.

Geographical Dictionary Test. page 115

OBJECTIVE The students will demonstrate their knowledge of the scope and limitations of a geographical dictionary.

SUGGESTIONS FOR USE Administer this test when your students have completed the activities in this unit.

ANSWERS *(Answers may vary.)*
A. 1. false **2.** true **3.** false **4.** true **5.** true **6.** true **7.** false **8.** false **9.** true
10. true
B. 1. 4,021 **2.** Hilo **3.** Captain Cook **4.** Sandwich Islands **5.** August 21, 1959